The Ethical Difference

The Ethical Difference

Why Leaders are More Than Managers

Joseph D. Potts

Copyright © 2001 by Joseph D. Potts.
All rights reserved. No part of this publication may be reproduced, stored in a retrieval system, or transmitted, in any form or by any means, electronic, mechanical, photocopying, recording, or otherwise, without the prior written permission of the publisher.

ROCKY MOUNTAIN PRESS

is a division of the

Rocky Mountain Institute for
Leadership Advancement
524 Emery Street
Longmont, CO 80501
1-888-709-0088
www.rmleadership.com

ORDERING INFORMATION:
For individual sales, quantity sales, and orders for college textbook/course adoption use contact the publisher at the address listed above.

Cover Design by Rebecca Luedders
Editing by Pauletta Raines

Printed in the United States of America

Library of Congress Control Number: 2001087891

ISBN 1-929149-09-3

for Sheryl

Contents

Note to the Reader 11
Preface 15

I   INTRODUCTION

Prologue 21

1   Leadership and Ethics 27

II   MANAGEMENT AND SURVIVAL

2   Worlds of Survival 37
    A Darwinian World: The Science of Survival 40
    The Organizational World:
        Survival of the Fittest Collective 44
    Public and Private: Divided We Live? 47
    The Nietzschean World: ~~*Survival*~~ *Superiority*
        of the ~~*Fittest*~~ *Few* 48
    Natural Science's Modern World:
        Nietzschean Darwinism? 53
    Concluding Unscientific Postscript 56

3   Managing to Survive 59
    The Meaning of "Is" 59
    Darwinian Management: The Science of Process 61
    Neo-Darwinian Supermanagement:
        Collective Superstition 64
    Nietzsche's Superman: The Will to Dominate 68
    Summary 73

III   LEADERSHIP AND PURPOSE

4 A World of Purpose   77
    Science and Purpose   77
    The Will to Meaning   80
    The Good is Common   83
    Success Re-Visioned   88

5 Leadership: ~~Survival~~ Service of the ~~Fittest~~ Faithful   93
    Back to Basics   93
    Clarifications and Implications   103
    The Mystical Mixture:
        Management, Influence, Leadership   105
    Transforming Influence   107
    The Story of Bill   110
    The Leader's Undivided World: Public and Private   114
    Practical Applications   120

IV   CONCLUSION

6 How Do Leaders Survive?   133
    How Do Leaders Survive?   133
    Reflections   138

Notes   145
Bibliography   155

Note to the Reader

Some years ago I had the opportunity to design and teach a college course called "Contemporary Issues in Leadership Studies." The third of three core courses in a new leadership studies field of emphasis, its main objective was to broaden students' understanding of leadership, building on the foundation of theory and practice that comprised the two introductory courses. Teachers often say they learn more in the classroom than do their students, and that was certainly my experience in this instance. Despite my plans to forge ahead to more "advanced" topics, class discussions kept circling back to rather basic questions. In particular, we kept returning to and wrestling with the working definition of leadership that students had learned in the first course. We kept going back to it because we could never quite nail down one basic concept: the distinction between management and leadership. This book is the fruit of a struggle that began then and continued for several semesters thereafter.

Early in my study and teaching of leadership, a person whose intelligence and integrity I greatly admire told me he saw relatively little that could be taught about leadership; certainly not enough could be said about it to justify an academic major or minor in the topic. Perhaps he was right. Leadership is not a subject that lends itself to course sequences of ever-increasing complexity, as with mathematics or chemistry. But this need not mean that we can't know, or shouldn't seek to clearly understand, what leadership is.

For one thing, leadership is eminently practical: it is something people do. Those who do leadership well may not always be able to define it in so many words, but others wishing to imitate them will be helped if they have some idea what they are looking for. This is especially true in an increasingly diverse, rapidly changing social environment, simply because there are fewer shared assumptions. In one sense, leadership is contingent upon cultural values or beliefs, and when those are in flux, the nature of leadership is harder to discern. Basic definitions then become more useful and necessary.

While not considering myself a particularly good leader, I have had the privilege of being around some outstanding ones. Also, I have at times been a fairly good follower, and if you've read anything about leadership in recent years you know that, at least according to some theorists, leadership and "followership" are best understood together, because leadership is something leaders and followers do together. If this is true, followers can indeed know something about leadership. The most valuable insight I have gained from my own experiences has to do with the difference between managing and leading. It is impossible to grasp leadership conceptually without a clear understanding of what distinguishes it from management.

Those with a genuine interest in leadership want to be able to clearly say who is a leader and who is not, or, at the very least, able to say when leadership is happening and when it is not. Those are *difficult* propositions because all leaders also manage to a greater or lesser extent. The trick is in knowing the difference. They are *important* propositions because not all managers do leadership, and when leadership is called for, we want to know whom to call upon. We want to be sure we call upon leaders, not just managers. The trick, again, is in knowing the difference.

Few would argue with the assertion that it is important to understand leadership. But why should doing so be difficult? Why not go along with the common assumption that leaders are essentially the managers at the top, and use the terms more or less interchangeably? I'm convinced that doing so is a serious mistake, and hope by the end of this book to have shown you why. I challenge you to read with pencil in hand, jotting reactions and questions in the margins. Whether you agree with my conclusions or not, I challenge you to be able to say why. Scholars may—no, will—continue to debate the meaning of leadership for decades to come, but those who wish to lead or follow *now* need a personal definition. What's yours?

Lawrence, Kan. J.D.P.
May 2001

Preface

One of the most useful things I learned in graduate school was also one of the simplest. It had to do with reading. The best teacher I've ever had, a professor of history named Robert Linder, impressed upon students in his graduate seminars two simple keys to understanding a book. You don't really understand a text, he declared, until you've identified both the author's thesis (his or her main point) and purpose (what he or she wanted to accomplish by writing the book). "Until you determine those two things," he said, "your judgment of a book has little merit."

With some books it is hard to pin those two things down. Not this book. My purpose is straightforward: I want to give persons who are interested in leadership something to think seriously about. My thesis is similarly straightforward: I argue that leadership can only be understood in ethical terms, but that management is best understood in non-ethical (but not *un*ethical) terms. My purpose is to offer a thought-provoking case for a particular way of understanding the difference between leadership and management. That case is based on the thesis that management has to do with survival, but leadership has to do with service.

So there you go, a purpose and a thesis. I will have achieved the former if I can get you to think hard about the latter. As to the latter, I believe it to be important for two reasons. First, despite the rapidly growing leadership literature, I've yet to see the points in this book stated plainly elsewhere, though they lurk just below the surface in the work of the best-known theorists, and seem to be logically essential to a correct understanding of what leadership is and what distinguishes it from management. Second, "leadership" is a word our society uses too much, and that overuse confuses our thinking about human behavior and reduces the potency of a vital concept. Like the word love, the word leadership is misused (and therefore abused) at least as often as not, and this misuse is ultimately the source of incalculable frustration and disillusionment. It is my hope that after reading this book, you will never again hear or say the word "leadership" without thinking about ethics; that you will test this book's thesis over and over in the months and years to come.

A Tactical Overview

The material in the following chapters is offered with two audiences in mind: academic readers with a theoretical orientation to leadership or management, and practitioners, those who are out there doing management or leadership and want to do one or both better. A conscious attempt has been made to keep the language reader-friendly throughout the book, but some parts will be of more interest to one group than the other.

The prologue provides for both groups a general orientation to the problem of distinguishing leadership from management. It then introduces a basic dichotomy around which the entire book is organized: the vast qualitative gulf separating the worlds of survival and purpose. Chapter One lays the groundwork for the academic elements of the book, reviewing key concepts from the work of the most influential contemporary scholars, and isolating important aspects of the definitions most widely accepted in the field at this time. Of primary importance here is the role of ethics in academic views of leadership. Practitioners may find the discussion of these definitions useful also, especially the intriguing differences between the ideas of two very important writers, J.M. Burns and Joseph Rost.

Chapter Two presents a broad consideration of the nature and implications of the Darwinian idea of survival of the fittest. The chapter reviews the development of "the survival paradigm" in the last two centuries, and contrasts it with its antithesis, the idea of purpose. At the same time, the chapter delineates several somewhat different ways of seeing the world, all of which are based on the survival paradigm. The chapter concludes by arguing that the survival idea presents difficult philosophical problems for would-be leaders. Chapter Three builds on Chapter Two by discussing implications of the survival paradigm for management. The chapter explores practical ways managers operate when the survival idea is fully embraced.

Chapter Four begins the second half of the book by laying a conceptual basis for understanding the world in terms of purpose as opposed to survival. Three concepts—meaning, the common good, and success—are discussed at some length because of their important place in the idea of leadership developed in Chapter Five. Chapters Four and Five both begin from more of an academic angle, but the latter half of each chapter includes a strong practical emphasis as well. Both also address the relationship between means and ends. Chapter Five distills the previous chapters into a working definition of leadership based on the premise that leadership is essentially a way of living ethically. Practitioners who are less interested in the academic argument will find an extended look at the practical implications of that premise in the latter half of the chapter.

Chapter Six briefly considers a few factors necessary for an individual to persevere in leadership over time and through difficult circumstances. It concludes by reflecting on the meaning of "leadership as ethics" in an academic sense and a personal sense.

Part I

INTRODUCTION

Do a little more of that work which you had sometime confessed to be good. — Thoreau

Prologue

O ye who lead, Take heed! Blindness we may forgive, but baseness we will smite.   – William Vaughn Moody

What We Need

A lot of books have already been written—some of them very good—on leadership. Some of the best are relatively recent scholarly works, products of the booming growth in academic programs offering degrees, certificates or minors in leadership studies. Students in these programs have an interest of one kind or another in "leadership," and a small minority have a burning desire to become leaders. The majority are simply on career tracks that will one day present them with managerial responsibilities in an organization of some kind, and just assume that leadership must be a part of such positions. They will read many scholarly works in the course of their programs. And their professors, no doubt, will continue to produce more books and articles for them to read.

This book offers additional food for thought to those students and professors, but also aims at those whose interest is purely practical because they are already in positions of responsibility. Such people don't have time to tackle a long, academic reading program, and are typically skeptical (often justifiably so) of ivory tower analyses of what for them is an intensely practical matter. At the same time, because it is such an immediate concern, they are continually interested in bettering their understanding of leadership. Whereas academics may not be all that concerned with nailing down "the" definition of leadership,[1] people in the trenches *must* do something akin to that. They need to know if they are indeed leaders—they need to know when they're leading, when they're managing, and how to tell the difference.

What We Want

Apart from the need to understand it better, what do people *want* leadership to be about? What do they want it to mean? Similar questions asked of other subjects are usually dismissed as missing the point. That is, asking what we *want* something to be or mean is generally, and usually rightly, understood to be irrelevant. Relevant questions are usually thought to be those along the lines of "What *is* it?" or, "What *are* we in fact dealing with?" Leadership is different. Important clues regarding its nature can be found in what people want it to be.

On the 26th of January, 1998, on live, national television, the President of the United States pointed his index finger directly at the American public and emphatically declared, "I want you to listen to me. I did not have sexual relations with that woman, Miss Lewinsky!" In so doing he offered a fundamental primer on the difference between management and leadership. Bill Clinton's actions that day were all about survival, but his survival—even the survival of political stability—was not what most people wanted, regardless of their choice of political party. It is not that they *didn't* want him to survive, for many did; what they wanted was to be told the truth. What they wanted was leadership. What they got, for want of a better word, was management.

This is not to say that management is always a bad thing. On the contrary, management is not only indispensable, it is absolutely unavoidable. But management and leadership are qualitatively different phenomena, and understanding leadership is difficult for the same reason that doing leadership is difficult. It is vastly more difficult to do than management. Management's goals are much clearer and more measurable; its failures are judged in terms less harsh. Management is evaluated in terms of efficiency, effectiveness and productivity, with "good" management resulting in more of each and "bad" management less. These judgments are morally neutral. For this reason, management is a simpler art than leadership. A manager's strategies, configurations or techniques work or do not work relative to clear, measurable goals, but morally, they are neither good nor bad.

Leadership doesn't get off of the hook that easily. Understanding and doing leadership are both difficult for one fundamental, defining reason: leadership is an ethical proposition. Ethical issues are always hard, and stated in the simplest terms possible, *leadership is ethics*. Actually, putting it that way both overstates and oversimplifies the case in several ways. But other ways of describing or defining the irreducible essence of leadership, while more complete and more technically correct, run the risk of drawing attention away from the most important distinction between leadership and management—the one thing that individuals who wish to lead or follow must keep in sharp focus. Fuller definitions of leadership are necessary, but are left aside now so as not to cloud the central argument. Leaders are held morally accountable, and their actions are therefore judged good or bad in the unavoidably idealistic terms of morality and purpose.

Over-complicated attempts to analyze it often cause confusion about leadership, but the bigger problem, by far, is daily language. The Greek language offers three different words for three distinct types of love; English squeezes them all into one. English gets by with one word for snow; the Inuit have many different ones for its various types and conditions. We might wish for something similar with leadership. The terms "leader" and "manager" are often used interchangeably, though we're really not sure that's a good thing. Down deep we sense we're missing a word or two, especially in cases like the one mentioned above. The term =="leader" can refer to a position in an organizational chart, or it can refer to a person who manifests a certain quality of character that is quite independent of his or her position.== These two meanings can cause a degree of ambiguity. How is it clearly implied or inferred that one meaning is intended but not the other? We feel we should call Bill Clinton something more than a manager, but hesitate to refer to him as a leader.

Until better words are invented, the best we can do is to try to be more careful. That is, we need to care more about the implications of the words we use. The motivation to do that might come from a better understanding of why leadership is more than management.

The Choices

Roughly 140 years before President Clinton's primer on management, Abraham Lincoln was conducting one on leadership. Lincoln's debates with Stephen Douglas boiled down to the question of *profit versus principle*. While Douglas saw the slavery question as one of economics, Lincoln saw it as a question of identity. For Douglas, each state "had the right to do as it pleased on the question of slavery, and every other question." He would proudly assert that "we of Illinois have decided it for ourselves. We tried slavery, kept it up for twelve years, and finding that it was not profitable we abolished it for that reason."[2]

Lincoln realized, however, that the American experiment was rooted in something much larger than profit. As one historian notes, Lincoln saw correctly that "the crucial premise" of the Declaration of Independence was that a nation could be built on an idea. In the case of the United States, that idea was the bedrock principle that "all men are created equal."[3] Push had finally come to shove. Abandoning that idea was suddenly a distinct possibility, but Lincoln knew that doing so would result in a union (or *dis*union) qualitatively different from, and morally inferior to, the one that existed before. The rest, as they say, is history.

Lincoln had declared in 1854 his hatred for the idea that "there is no right principle of action but self-interest."[4] Ironically, only five years later an English naturalist published a book that unintentionally but starkly illuminated the central issue of the Lincoln-Douglas debates. In his *Origin of Species*, Charles Darwin described the competitive struggle for survival that naturally selected the strongest or most advantaged of any given species. Concisely formulating the antithesis of Lincoln's position, Darwin identified self-interest as the *only* principle of action.

Speaking from the ranks of the most advantaged, Douglas wanted simply to do what worked; Lincoln wanted more. Douglas wanted the United States to manage; Lincoln wanted it to lead.

1

Leadership and Ethics

In central China, high above the Yellow River near the ancient city of Zhengzhou, a famous poem from the Tang dynasty is carved into the face of a cliff. Translated from Mandarin to English, the poem reads something like this:

> The sun sinks slowly behind the mountains
> The Yellow River flows to the sea
> If you want to be able to see everything
> Climb higher.

The message is simple but powerful. The poet reminds us that the world is a big place, and if we want to see further—if we want to see more than we can see now—we must seek a higher vantage point. Put more colloquially, we have to step back.

"Stepping back" and surveying things that have been written about leadership in recent years yields at least three observations. First, most if not all such writers, no matter what or how much else they have to say, refer to James MacGregor Burns' masterly 1978 study, *Leadership*. Burns's book won a Pulitzer Prize, but in fact one particular idea in the book—a category of leadership Burns labeled "transforming"—has been the focus of this lasting interest. In words now quite familiar to every other scholar in the field, he defined this as a kind of leadership that "ultimately becomes moral in that it raises the level of human conduct and ethical aspiration of both the leader and the led."[1] The second observation is that a large majority of writers give some degree of attention to values or ethics. Third, nearly every writer mentions Robert Greenleaf's captivating 1977 book, *Servant Leadership*, somewhere along the line. Greenleaf's "servant-leader" is fundamentally concerned with seeking the good by serving others.[2]

A quick survey of book titles from the past twelve years illustrates the point being made here. *Values Leadership* (Fairholm), *Leadership and the Quest for Integrity* (Badaracco and Ellsworth), *The Ethical Imperative* (Dalla Costa), *Character: America's Search for Leadership* (Sheehy), and *Lives of Moral Leadership* (Coles) are just a few. Ethics and morality have become important topics for people who study leadership. The question to be asked, then, is whether or not this is a good thing. Is it appropriate for so much attention to be given to this most controversial of subjects?

The title of one book in particular offers an unequivocal response. *Ethics, the Heart of Leadership* is a collection of articles by top leadership theorists examining from various perspectives the relationship between leadership and ethics. Editor Joanna Ciulla indeed believes, as her title indicates, that ethics is the "heart" of leadership.[3] Some people who are supposed to know say that she's right. Burns is one. Another reviewer says Ciulla's book "takes the big leap forward" because it tackles issues that are central to leadership but have largely been avoided.[4] But is she, in fact, *right*? Is leadership truly a "moral activity?" Commenting on her book, another respected scholar points to this as "the single most important question" in the study of leadership.[5]

This book unreservedly agrees with that statement, as well as with the spirit of Ciulla's assertion that ethics is "the heart of leadership." She is correct in observing that, although scholars and practitioners of leadership "genuflect at the altar of ethics" and speak with "hushed reverence" about its importance, there has been no sustained, systematic treatment of this supposedly essential dimension.[6] This is an astute and absolutely accurate observation. In most discussions of leadership to date (even those by several of the contributors to her book), those doing the discussing have not fully addressed the implications of the idea that ethics is somehow the "heart" or "soul" of leadership. This may be because the practice-oriented interest in leadership today generally slants toward the business world, where ethics usually has a particular but limited meaning for those who think it important, and no meaning at all for those of the bare-knuckles school who think it largely irrelevant. Whatever the reason, writers have yet to step back far enough to ponder what such an idea might really mean.

It means a lot. Current discussions assume that the term "ethics" means the same to all who hear or use it. At most, some effort is made to distinguish "ethics" from "morals" or to explain how "ethical values" differ from other kinds of values.[7] More tellingly, these assumptions and distinctions generally occur in considerations of leadership as it pertains to an organization or group. Ethics is then implicitly limited by the same parameters, and related only to leaders' interactions with groups.

Stepping back calls these approaches into question. Properly understood, ethics is a sub-discipline which cannot be comprehended if separated from its parent discipline, which is *philosophy*.[8] The other two sub-disciplines, or other two categories of philosophic inquiry, are epistemology, having to do with the nature of knowledge, and metaphysics, having to do with first principles and ultimate reality.[9] Of course, there are those for whom even the mention of philosophy is a signal to high-tail it in the opposite direction. Still others are simply interested in "getting work done" rather than, as philosophers are often characterized, "just thinking about work." Their point is well-taken. These negative connotations notwithstanding, we cannot deny that ethics—the study of morals and moral problems—is a category of philosophy.

But, what is philosophy? Consider these answers from three famous thinkers:

> *Aristotle*: philosophers "are seeking the first principles and highest causes…"
> *Plato*: a philosopher is "the spectator of all time and all existence."
> *Ludwig Wittgenstein*: the philosopher's aim is "to show the fly the way out of the fly bottle."[10]

Ethics, because it is a category of philosophy, must be understood in similar terms. First, when evaluating potential choices, ethicists are seeking the *highest* good, not just the good of one group. They assume that "the good" is higher than other possible pursuits, and that "the good life" is better than other lives that might be imagined or currently experienced. Also, this "good life" is defined in terms of *all* time and *all* people; that is, it is understood to apply universally. Ethical principles are not free-floating axioms that can be mixed, matched, or used piecemeal, divorced from a larger system of belief. Individual ethical principles spring from a vision of the whole of human experience, and are therefore meant to apply in some way to all groups. Finally, ethicists are interested in finding out how to reach that good life. They are interested in *practice*. Ethics, then, is concerned with an all-encompassing understanding of what is good or right, and with how to get there. For these reasons, it is concerned with something referred to herein as "the common good."

Having made these points about the nature of philosophy and ethics, let us then return to our starting point. Joanna Ciulla has stated her belief that ethics is the heart of leadership, and well-respected scholars have agreed with her. But could one effectively argue in a relatively brief space that such an assertion has merit?

At least in theoretical terms, this is not hard to do. One need only turn to current definitions. Granted, definitions are chosen from among alternatives, and the correctness of such choices can always be challenged. But if one or more assumptions are present in the core definitions—that is, within the current paradigm—of a given field of inquiry, a question like the one just asked can be meaningfully answered.[11] In this case, we can look to see if broadly accepted definitions of leadership assume that ethics plays a vital role—at least as far as the definitions themselves go. Most leadership scholars today work within a paradigm heavily influenced first by Burns and then by another important theorist, Joseph Rost. What do we find in their definitions?

Burns, as noted earlier, is a focus of continuing interest because of what he identified as a *type* of leadership (*transforming leadership*), distinctive in that it "morally elevates" both leaders and followers, and is concerned with ethical "end values" such as liberty, justice, or equality.[12] Burns' definition of transforming leadership, noted above, has become a fixture in the leadership literature. Though never intended to be a comprehensive definition for all types of leadership, many see this particular aspect of Burns' analysis as most compelling. It has thus heavily influenced the current leadership paradigm, and because of its essential ethical dimension, can therefore be considered strong evidence in support of Ciulla's assertion.

Transforming leadership is now accepted, as Burns apparently intended, as one important type of leadership—perhaps the most important—but not as an umbrella term for all types of leadership. He did offer a comprehensive definition as well, but it has not received the same level of attention.[13] Rost's comprehensive definition, on the other hand, is a different story. Rost outlined his paradigm-altering view of leadership in a 1990 book entitled *Leadership for the Twenty-First Century*. After a thorough, probing review of the history and past uses of the term, Rost asserted that leadership should be generally and best defined as "an influence relationship between leaders and followers who intend real changes that reflect their mutual purposes."[14]

Rost's view is important here for three reasons. First, it has gained much attention but has so far stood up as being broadly viable. Second, it is comprehensive in that it attempts to encompass all possible types and manifestations of leadership. Third, it is complementary to Burns in that it affirms a particular "modal" or "means" value, as opposed to Burns' emphasis on "end" values in his discussion of transforming leadership.[15] Rost's definition implicitly invokes the ethical principle of respect for human dignity as an essential element of the leader–follower relation.

The third point deserves additional attention. Rost makes this implicit element explicit in his book, stating that the operation of leadership depends on this ethical principle. In his words, leadership "adds to the autonomy and value of the individuals in the relationship. Leadership does not require that individuals sacrifice some of their integrity to be in the relationship."[16] In short, per Rost, leadership hinges on the operation of a specific ethical value or principle, rather than on the pursuit of an ethical end or goal. In fact, Rost strenuously objects to the idea that ethical ends can in any way be a necessary component of leadership.[17] But ethicality of means, or process, is for him a different matter. If the particular ethical principle of human autonomy is violated, leadership is not happening. At least with respect to process, no ethics means no leadership. With respect to process, leadership is ethical by nature.

So, albeit in very different ways, two extremely influential contemporary theorists lend significant support to Ciulla's assertion that ethics is the "heart" of leadership. Burns affirms ethical ends; Rost affirms ethical means. We could add to them Greenleaf's servant leader idea, which consistently receives attention in the leadership literature and is in itself a wholesale operationalizing of ethical assumptions. His ideal of service is measured by the extent to which those served "become healthier, wiser, freer, more autonomous," and by whether or not "the least privileged in society" benefit from, or are at least not harmed by, that service.[18] This is leadership as ethics *par excellence*.

The question, then, is so what? If Ciulla is right, why belabor the matter? Is her own book not an extended discussion of the significance of ethics? Yes and no. Yes, in that all of the articles in the book, including her own, address the operation of ethics in leadership in one form or another. The fundamental problem, however, is failure to do the reverse. That is, the articles fail to address the location of leadership *within* ethics.

For Ciulla, leadership without ethics has no heart. Without ethics, perhaps, leadership does not occur at all. But if ethics has to do with what is universally good (or the "common good" as it is referred to herein), and if leadership is an ethical activity, then leadership cannot be divorced from such good. *In philosophical terms, leadership is best understood as one way of living an ethical life; it is ethical living involving others in certain relational ways.* It is a form of ethical expression, ethical living writ large. As a category, then, leadership theory is subsumed within ethics. Put a little differently, the potential weight of this whole line of argument becomes plain: persons who pursue goals other than the goal of the common good are not doing leadership. Whatever they may be doing, they are not leading.

And just what might those persons be doing? Fair question, and one whose answer will occupy a good portion of the next few chapters. For now, the point is more basic. A credible argument can be made to support the assertion that leadership, as currently defined, is somehow bound together with the common good.

But what is that? Perhaps the most remarkable omission in current writing on leadership is the almost total absence of cogent, in-depth discussions of the idea of the common good. In fairness, on the other hand, if one takes the view (as does Rost) that the common good—or any other *end* good—is not an essential concern for leaders, then such an omission is to be expected. Whatever the reasons, the leadership literature lacks well-considered discussions of the common good. Chapter Four takes up this problem briefly.

But what are we to call those activities that do not serve the common good? More "stepping back" is required to find an answer, for we need to gain a basic grasp of the context. Just as ethics must be situated within the context of philosophy, leadership and management must be situated within the context of human activity in general. It is to that context we first turn our attention.

Before doing so, there is a challenge to be presented. Those who have studied or read about leadership are likely to be familiar with the timeworn illustration of a group of people needing to find their way out of a dense forest. Leaders, according to the illustration, are those who climb to the top of tall trees and point the group in the right direction. Managers are those individuals in charge of the logistics of moving the group in the specified direction. Managers keep the group together while working around and through the trees. Knowledge of group psychology and familiarity with trees, however, reveal precious little about the larger forest, to say nothing of what might lie beyond it. In the illustration, it is the leader's job to know forests.

If a single weakness of most contemporary writing about leadership had to be identified, this would be it. Trees, so to speak, and group process are in vogue, and lots of books are being written about these topics. Few authors seem to have the time or the interest necessary to understand the bigger picture. "Forests" have largely been forgotten, and we are worse off as a result. No one can claim to understand subtraction without an understanding of mathematics. And no one can claim to understand leadership unless they can also present—with appropriate humility and respect—a coherent, overarching understanding of the environment of human thought and behavior within which leadership occurs. It is odd that we think we can lead without knowing where we are going or, worse yet, without believing we are in fact going anywhere at all.

Part II

MANAGEMENT AND SURVIVAL

A very ordinary life—an average income, a little soldiering, a good deal of sport whenever sport offered, plenty of friends, plenty of pleasant things to do, a sufficiency of women. The kind of life that practically inhibits thought of any description and substitutes sensation. To speak frankly, an animal's life. – Agatha Christie

2

Worlds of Survival

This survival of the fittest...is that which Mr. Darwin has called "natural selection, or the preservation of favored races in the struggle for life."
— Herbert Spencer

When "climbing higher" in an attempt to see the entire panorama of behavior within which leadership occurs, we discover something interesting. Upon reaching a suitably lofty vantage point, we find that we are not alone. Others were there ahead of us, and they are busy watching the action, surveying the entirety of human experience, taking notes, and discussing with one another what they see. Interestingly, these observers have divided themselves into two groups, and though from time to time they shout remarks back and forth (which sometimes are not very nice), the two groups pretty much ignore one another. On rare occasions, isolated individuals do change groups. But as we go first to one group and introduce ourselves, and then to the other, both are congenial and don't mind when we listen in on their conversations.

It takes some time, but eventually we figure out that the groups have separated from one another because they sharply disagree as to how best to explain the animal and human activity going on below them. There are scientists in both groups, but one group is clearly dedicated to using only scientific terminology as they describe and attempt to explain behavior. They seem to be significantly more unified as a group than do the others, apparently because they all agree upon one particular concept. They have a great deal of faith in the concept, and are confident that it is a dependable starting point. From it, they use deductive reasoning to explain the things they see taking place. That concept has something to do with survival. Interestingly, when we inform them that we have come up to try and learn something about leadership, they aren't sure what to say. Finally one asks, "Do you mean management?" But they welcome us to observe with them anyway.

The other group is less unified. It seems to include quite a few philosophers and theologians. There are plenty of scientists mixed in, too, but the language of choice is not particularly scientific. They disagree with one another on lots of issues, and frequently get into heated debates. Still, the group somehow hangs together. It takes a while to figure this one out, because even when we ask, many of them aren't able to get right to the point. Some of them don't have a lot of confidence in their views, and so keep qualifying everything they say. But we persist, and finally it dawns on us: in one way or another, all of these people are talking about purpose. When we tell them of our interest in leadership, they all nod their heads. One smiles and replies, "Oh, we've all got opinions on that!"

****

Each organic being...at some period of its life, during some season of the year...has to struggle for life and to suffer great destruction.... From the war of nature, from famine and death, the most exalted object which we are capable of conceiving, namely, the production of the higher animals, directly follows. There is grandeur in this view of life...having been originally breathed by the Creator into a few forms or into one...
– Charles Darwin

While the law [of competition] may sometimes be hard for the individual, it is best for the race, because it insures the survival of the fittest in every department. We accept and welcome, therefore, as conditions to which we must accommodate ourselves, great inequality of environment, the concentration of business, industrial and commercial, in the hands of a few, and the law of competition between these, as being not only beneficial, but essential for the future progress of the race.
– Andrew Carnegie

A people is nature's detour to arrive at six or seven great men...
– Friedrich Nietzsche

An understanding of the human experience begins with the question of whether it is best described in terms of a struggle for survival or in light of some kind of overarching purpose. One's position on this question will have a lot to do with what one thinks about leadership, because leadership necessarily occurs within some sort of context. That is, our view of leadership makes sense only insofar as it is consistent with our view of the world. If we endorsed the survival paradigm but also wanted to lead, our task would be to lead in a context defined by that paradigm, probably similar to one or more of those described below. We would have to be able to explain what leadership means in such contexts.

A Darwinian World: The Science of Survival

Upon hearing of Charles Darwin's theory of natural selection, in particular the proposing of human descent from non-human primates, a contemporary of his remarked, "Let's hope that it's not true; and if it is true, let's hope that it does not become widely known."[1] Lady Ashley hoped in vain, for Darwin probably has more name recognition among the general population than any other scientist heretofore. Moreover, the average person on the street knows and can correctly attribute to him (though the actual phrase came originally from Spencer) his most basic axiom, survival of the fittest.

Darwin's remarkable renown has a simple explanation: it is because his central principle is so easy to grasp. Everyone sees it in operation everywhere; many have experienced it first-hand. From the quotations above, Spencer's "struggle," Carnegie's "competition" and Darwin's "war" resonate immediately with all but those living the most sheltered of lives. Leaving aside questions related to origins and transitional forms, natural selection has been profoundly useful to biologists and sociologists as they attempt to describe what goes on in the world of organisms. Most of all, it highlights and explains a central reality of that world—the struggle for survival.

Although it now seems odd to the Western mind, pre-Enlightenment thought assumed the role of purpose in all fields of study, including chemistry, physics, and astronomy. To us, it seems obvious that chemical reactions or the movement of planets in orbit can be described without reference to any sort of "purpose." But Greek science saw motion as inexplicable unless it was purposive, a "movement from the less good to the good."[2] What seems to be common sense to us represented a monumental breakthrough in the sixteenth and seventeenth centuries. Isaac Newton was the key figure in this leap, discovering and describing fundamental, unvarying physical laws as the key to explaining the movements of physical bodies. Eliminating purpose as a methodological component in the fields of physics and astronomy signaled the birth of modern science, and opened the door to enormous changes in perspective. Adding gravity to the picture, for example, changed the picture a *lot*. "Hitherto," said Newton, "we have explained the phenomena of the heavens and of our sea..."[3]

As Newton was to physical science, so Darwin was to behavioral science. As gravity explained the movements of inanimate objects, so the struggle to survive seemed to effectively explain the movements of animate ones. Evolutionary psychologist David Buss summarizes many scientists' view of the sweeping explanatory power of Darwin's theory in this way:

> Ancestral selection pressures are responsible for creating the...strategies we use today.... Within each person's life, social and physical environments provide input to the evolved psychological mechanisms, and *every behavior is without exception* a joint product of those mechanisms and their environmental influences."[4] (italics added)

Despite this explanatory power, however, Buss acknowledges that the grim reality Darwinian theory embraces has been one barrier to its acceptance. One opposing view of human nature sees our "natural" state as one of peaceful, harmonious coexistence with plants, animals and one another.[5] But after conducting the most massive study of human mating behavior ever, involving more than 10,000 people from 37 cultures worldwide, Buss challenges us to be more clear-eyed than that. "Much of what I discovered...is not nice. In the ruthless pursuit of sexual goals, for example, men and women derogate their rivals, deceive members of the opposite sex, and even subvert their own mates."[6]

Such an assessment is neither new nor unusual. Political philosopher Thomas Hobbes published the classic treatise on humanity's natural state in 1651. *Leviathan*'s thirteenth chapter is famously blunt. In the absence of the coercive power of the state, Hobbes asserted, mankind's natural condition is anything but idyllic. It is essentially a state of war, characterized by "...continual fear, and danger of violent death; and the life of man, solitary, poor, nasty, brutish, and short."[7]

Inhabitants of the modern West may protest that human nature really isn't *that* bad anymore, but Hobbes anticipated such objections. Do we lock our doors at night? Do we have locked "chests" inside our homes as well, even though we know there is a local police department? "Do you by these actions," he asked, "not accuse your fellow man just as do my words?" The much sought-after ideal of equality proves in the end to be of little comfort, Hobbes said, because equality only means that people can never feel safe from "invasion." Peace at home can only be the product of a "contract" among citizens, refereed by the coercive power of a strong central government, under which they mutually renounce their power to kill, enslave, and steal from one another. Outside national borders, the "state of nature" prevails whenever unmitigated by effective international authority. Nations are "in the state and posture of Gladiators; having their weapons pointing; and their eyes fixed on one another; that is, their Forts, Garrisons, and Guns...; and continual Spyes upon their neighbors...."[8] Three and a half centuries ago, Hobbes described the Cold War to a tee.

— Westerners have quickly forgotten what the state of nature is and how close to the surface it may be. Too few of us have read *The Price of Glory*, Alistair Horne's penetrating look at World War One. The forgetfulness is particularly characteristic of Americans, because our wars in the last century were fought at a distance, Pearl Harbor being the arguable exception. Unless, of course, one is familiar with the reality of America's inner cities. For their inhabitants, as for millions upon millions of others around the world, the state of nature is a matter of daily experience. Raw capitalism in the post-Marxian former Soviet Union has rapidly led to conditions similar to the Hobbesian vision, and things are only slightly better in some parts of present-day China. A December 2000 Associated Press wire story reported 68 countries, more than a third of all countries in the world, suffering from civil unrest, drug wars and other conflicts. This number is up from 65 a year earlier, and is nearly twice the average at the time superpower rivalry ended ten years prior to that.[9] Hobbes apparently knew what he was talking about; we seem to have proven his point for him.

Some will protest that the case is too easily overstated, that cynical views are too easily disguised as "objectivity." Philosopher Christopher Hodgkinson reminds us, however, of the strength of arguments for a negative view of life, a view bluntly stated in the Buddha's First Noble Truth: life is suffering. In response to the counter that life also contains pleasures and delights, the Buddhist responds that "all pleasures are themselves tainted sources of suffering for they are transient, fleeting, consummated only in the knowledge that they are passing, leaving behind as traces only the seeds of craving for painful repetition."[10] Contemporary bumper stickers are more succinct: "Life's a bitch, and then you die." Or, "He who dies with the most toys, wins." And its rejoinder, "He who dies with the most toys, still dies."

But we are jumping ahead too quickly. It is important to note that neither Darwin (at least initially) nor even Hobbes shared such thoroughly pessimistic sentiments. It is often forgotten that Hobbes was a theist who believed that a civil society of sorts could be constructed as an antidote to the horrors of human nature, and his Protestant faith provided a purpose for doing so. And, at least in the conclusion of his *Origin of Species*, Darwin presented himself as an optimist, a materialist of faith who saw direction in the natural struggle of living creatures. That struggle gradually improved things, and survival, therefore, was an end in itself. He affirmed that "natural selection works solely by and for the good of each being, [and] all corporeal and mental endowments will tend to progress towards perfection."[11] Julian Huxley later described Darwin's vision as having provided a "glorious opportunity...to promote the maximum fulfillment of the evolutionary process on the earth."[12]

Darwin recognized the brutality of natural struggle, but his science did not prevent him from holding out hope. Yes, things were rough, especially on individuals, but the end result would be good for many. People could draw at least a modicum of comfort from this analysis. For one thing, the war of existence—Hobbes's world—had a scientific explanation. For another, it was leading somewhere better; it wasn't just a simple matter of might making right. Nature had good intentions.

The Organizational World: Survival of the Fittest Collective

As sociologist Max Weber, theologian Jacques Ellul, and management guru Peter Drucker predicted, western society has become "organizational," with our lives affected and governed by the actions of increasingly large and complex organizations. Hodgkinson believes western society can now be described as "neo-feudal" because the dominant relationship for an individual within it is his or her primary organizational affiliation. The "new fiefdoms" are those of the great institutions: large-scale, often transnational corporations in the private sector, complex bureaucracies in the public sector, and the oligopolies and cartels of semi-regulated capitalism. The new "liege lords" are the managerial and executive elite. There are thousands of smaller fiefdoms as well, with their own lesser liege lords.

What is life like within and between modern organizations? We might hope that the organizations which characterize and dominate the modern world, and with which most of us are affiliated in some way, would shield us from the rough and tumble of nature, but arguments to the contrary are close at hand. Hodgkinson's summary of a Hobbesian-Darwinian view of life inside modern organizations merits quoting at length.

> At it's lowest level [life in organizations] is hedonic, [as] men seek to gain pleasure and avoid pain...to maximize their own welfare within a set of game rules or constraints...provided by the organization to which they owe their allegiance and within which they play out their games. If [they are in fact] in it for what they can get out of it...it can lead to an ethics of the trough. Life, played out through the forms of organizational careers, is a struggle, by hand and mind, of each against all for

a better place at the trough, a better share of the rewards-system pie, a ruthless but covert pursuit of self-interest within the organization game, a steady and relentless effort to maximize perquisites, power and status, which ends only with ultimate expulsion from the organization by dismissal or retirement (or else by transfer, voluntary or forced, to another organizational context where [the] battle continues)....

[O]rganizations can be construed as moral primitives...[but] because only an individual can possess consciousness and will...organizations cannot be morally responsible. Nevertheless organizations are collectively more powerful than individuals and they do act in the world. Though such action be directed to ostensibly benevolent ends its potential for corruption cannot be ignored.... Organizations are not conscious. They cannot feel. Though potent they are faceless.[13]

Much more could be said here, and opposing views could also be considered. But the possibility that Hodgkinson's description is accurate would logically seem to lead organizers to use caution and sensitivity as they build organizations. Indeed, many authorities apparently assume that organizations as they are now structured are essentially benevolent, and that the achievement of organizational goals and growth of capital outweigh any costs to individuals inside and entities outside. There is plenty of evidence to the contrary. Managers, leaders, and those who aspire to be one or the other need to read carefully here, for it can be convincingly argued that this is the stuff of life in modern organizational society.

[Researchers] Scott and Hart...have analyzed the concept of the organizational imperative. This is specified as being made up of two propositions and three ethical values. The two propositions are: *'Whatever is good for the individual can only come from the modern organization,'* and therefore, *'All behaviour must enhance the health of such organizations.'* The three ethical rules are: *the rule of rationality* (the task of administration is to maximize efficiency defined as the ratio of output to input); *the rule of stewardship* (administrators owe primary loyalty to the [organization]); and *the rule of pragmatism* (administrators must be expedient and must focus on short-term reality to the exclusion of long-term idealism).[14]

(italics added)

Whether or not one agrees with Scott and Hart, one cannot deny that organizations are dominant actors in the world today. Accordingly, books on leadership or management today focus almost exclusively on various types of activity within organizational contexts. Most authors assume that organizations, like individuals, have a right to struggle for survival, and struggle they do. Corporate warfare and hostile takeovers vividly illustrate how well organizations fit in a Darwinian world.

There are many that would prefer some other description of life, but formulating an argument against natural selection is no simple task. The survival paradigm is formidable, and so far it has been fit enough to survive as a picture of both natural and organizational life. Most compelling for leaders and managers in the modern West is the point, worth repeating here, that Hobbes' state of nature is a day-to-day reality for many in the world today. Modern organizations in the West, or at least their corporate headquarters, mediate and condition that reality for their members and clients, providing explicit and implicit rules for the game as it is to be played within the organization, and providing on-site referees to oversee the game. But those provisions are purchased at the price of allegiance to the organization.

Thus ends our thumbnail sketch of the Darwinian "forest." It leaves us with a number of unanswered questions and, perhaps, a longing for a more uplifting synopsis of human activity. Before attempting to address those questions, however, two subordinate "forests" need to be identified. Darwin apparently said nothing about them, but they had begun to take shape in the century before him, and are now common in modern life. No description of the context within which management and leadership take place is complete without them.

Public and Private: Divided We Live?

Industrial society and the rise of organizations within it have given birth to another pair of worlds: the public and the private. Life in earlier societies was generally characterized by individual families and small communities using farming or various skilled crafts to sustain themselves. Society changed radically when work was removed from the home to the factory. The home was no longer the place of work, and the family was no longer the working unit. As one writer puts it, a "deep divide" opened between the public world "of work, of exchange, of economics, and the private world."[15]

In the public world, employees might or might not know one another's names, and began to serve as replaceable units in mechanical processes. At home, in the private world, individuals were "known to one another as irreplaceable persons, and their mutual understanding as persons" was what constituted the home.[16] Changes in social geography further exacerbated the dichotomy. Mechanization led to urbanization as a result of the need to concentrate large numbers of workers, which in turn gradually replaced traditional family-based communities with a number of overlapping networks, each serving different purposes.

Also, where work and the products of work had formerly been seen to have immediate, real value to the communities within which they arose, capitalism inaugurated a never-ending cycle of production simply for the sake of consumption. Products that met no genuine need were generated in mass quantities with planned obsolescence for faceless masses of end consumers. Consumers, in turn, were endlessly propagandized by advertising. In raw terms, economics came into being as "market science," which assumed that the market was a self-operating mechanism somewhat like the Newtonian universe. Its fundamental governing law stated that covetousness was the basic drive of human nature.[17] That drive and the market it generated were not immoral, they just were, and participation in it—despite the alienation of producer from consumer and the increasing meaninglessness of production—became unavoidable. Like gravity and other Newtonian laws, the law of the market was accepted as a morally neutral "fact of life." Production became a public activity having no personal dimension.

Also significantly, modern science contributed to the public-private schism by assuming that all human activity, not just in the economic realm, could be described in terms of such facts. The public world—the "real," "factual" world—thus came to be seen as independent of the private world of faith, value, or purpose. Purpose and meaning were classified as individual, private constructions, and because they did not exist in the objective physical and behavioral universe of science, were seen to have no necessary place in it.

Rather than being rooted in a single community network encompassing work, leisure, family relationships, and religion, individuals are confronted by modern public life with multiple possibilities and a plurality of worlds. A social environment where public and private were melded within a given world accepted as real, offering individuals a constant place and well-defined identity, has generally been replaced by neighbors who move in so they can work somewhere outside the neighborhood, and are likely to move back out again in two to four years. Neighbors often worship different gods (if any at all), and rarely have any necessary relationship with one another. In a very real way, personal identity is up for grabs. Needs for intimacy and security are to be fulfilled at home, in the private world.

The Nietzschean World: ~~Survival~~ Superiority of the ~~Fittest~~ Few

As often as not, philosophy as a discipline seems impractical and irrelevant to the average person. A common response to a speaker or text somehow identified as philosophical is therefore to "tune it out." But philosophy in its simplest terms is just an attempt to figure out and describe what's really going on in the world. German philosopher Friedrich Nietzsche took his place in the natural order soon after Darwin, and gave an account of what was going on that was somewhat different from Darwin's. Nietzsche's take on the big picture soon overshadowed those of all his peers and predecessors, and profoundly influenced the thinking of many who came after him.[18]

Writing in the latter half of the nineteenth century, Nietzsche believed he stood at the end of an old world and at the beginning of a new one. Some credit him with a part in the founding of that new world, but Nietzsche maintained that he was simply describing, albeit before anyone else, processes that were already in full swing. He agreed with Hobbes and Darwin that history was brutal, that the realities of natural struggle were often grim. He disagreed with them in two significant ways, however.

First, things were worse than they had been portrayed, and would soon become even more so. Second, there was no purpose and no grand scheme to lend coherence to the world. Nietzsche believed that ideas of purpose—both natural purpose ala Darwin and the contrived purpose of religion—would finally and necessarily give way to a world of no meaning at all: human history as a sequence of events guided neither by purpose or underlying laws. The immediate result would be destruction and violence on a scale never before seen.[19] Whatever the causes, he was right about the effects. In the first 60 years of the twentieth century—the 60 years following Nietzsche's death—28 million people, more than all of those dying on battlefields in the 19 preceding centuries combined, would die in European wars or at the hands of totalitarian regimes.

Nietzsche was 15 years old when England's Darwin published *The Origin of Species*. Twenty-three years later, having given the book some thought, Nietzsche published a position in response.

> There is a fundamentally erroneous doctrine in contemporary morality, celebrated particularly in England: according to this, the judgments "good" and "evil" are condensations of [the] "expedient" and "inexpedient"; what is called good preserves

the species, while what is called evil is harmful to the species....[20]

In Nietzsche's judgment, the desire for self-preservation only manifested itself when an organism was under distress. Conditions of distress, however, are rare in nature. More common, he said, are conditions of overflow to the point of squandering. When encountered, distressing conditions are only a temporary restriction of the will to life. Rather than survival, therefore, the most fundamental instinct is the desire for "expansion of power." To fulfill this instinct, individuals will risk, and sometimes forego, self-preservation. Therefore, the most important struggles always revolve around power, and the use of it to grow, expand, and attain superiority. To Nietzsche, the real will of life was "the will to power." Every aspect of human behavior, except when under distress, could be explained by the desire for self-assertion. He saw Darwinism as an "incomprehensibly one-sided doctrine" because it ignored the importance of the desire for power.[21] In the average human, however, he believed this desire was weakened into a contemptible desire for security, prosperity, and bliss.

The way Nietzsche developed the "other side" he saw missing in Darwin's thought is directly relevant to the study of management and leadership. Where Darwin saw individuals in service to the species, Nietzsche saw species in the service of individuals. The species in general, he felt, was *not* making progress, and really didn't need to. In fact, democracy and general education were serving to smother the few individuals who carried the burden of true progress: the "Single Ones."[22] These individuals, the "overmen" or "supermen," would fulfill in their persons the highest dreams of what was possible for the human race. These higher individuals would be laws unto themselves, answering to no one and desiring no followers. "He shall be the greatest who can be the loneliest, the most hidden, the most deviating, the human being beyond good and evil, the master of his virtues..."[23] But where and when necessary, the supermen would impose their wishes on the masses of average beings around them, for the masses were eager to kneel in submission before anyone with a true will to power. Progress, then, was not measured by the development of a species as a whole, but by the strong ones who emerged from within a species, sometimes to dominate it.

The other aspect of Nietzsche's thought that is important here has to do with purpose. Nietzsche saw traditional religious morality as a hindrance to great individuals; such morality was "the instinct of the herd against the strong and independent ones." It opposed the happy ones who successfully created their *own* law. But in his day, Nietzsche saw traditional confidence in religion rapidly giving way to "an unlimited faith in scientific progress."[24] Such progress was helping the average person, at heart only a beast, achieve the crude goals of safety, security, entertainment and amusement, things quite inferior to the promises of religion. Higher values could now be left behind. The supermen had always known such values were false, but among the masses and the possessing classes, the results of this loss of foundation would be catastrophic. The death of God would result in an incredible sequence of terrors in "a warlike age," but the supermen would not be dismayed by the dark times to come. Rather, they looked forward to the coming catastrophes as they would the light of dawn after a long night. Now that "the old god" was dead, their hearts overflowed "with gratitude, amazement, anticipation, expectation" because a great hindrance had been removed. Daring searches by lovers of knowledge would be permitted again.[25]

In a Nietzschean world, these searches serve no purpose beyond the personal fulfillment of the few individuals brave enough to "live dangerously." These rare persons have the strength to live without God and without transcendent purpose, and are able to renounce even happiness if their uniqueness demands it. The "great ones" can manipulate or impose their will on the masses when they wish, because they "can afford not only the *sight* of the terrible and the questionable, but even the terrible deed and any luxury of destruction." For these superior representatives of humanity, "what is evil, senseless, and ugly" seems permissible, as it is permissible in the natural world, if necessary to an act of artistic creation.[26] Such is the nature of genuine achievement. As to the masses themselves, the progress most seek amounts to nothing more than a mellowing of their "hostile instincts."[27]

Nietzsche's strange, disturbing vision of the world would seem to be of little practical relevance in a discussion of modern management or leadership but for two factors: his remarkable insights into the nature of science and scientific thinking, and his provocative analysis of human mediocrity and greatness. With regard to the adequacy of the survival paradigm, these two aspects of Nietzsche's work are penetrating.

Nietzsche's ideas of greatness are instructive in several ways, but especially with regard to their influence and outworking in the life of Adolf Hitler. Hitler's name inevitably comes up in classroom debates regarding the nature of leadership. Was Hitler a leader? Someone is sure to ask. In point of fact, Burns's foreword to Ciulla's book on ethics and leadership begins and ends with this very classroom scenario. For the moment, we can note Hitler's full assent to the Darwinian view. He understood war to be "a test of national will and character," a struggle that only the fittest would survive. But he added a distinctly Nietzschean twist. Against democratic notions, and especially against the Marxist idea of the "triumph of the many," he opposed "the Aristocratic principle of Nature" and "the privilege of power."[28] Only the few that were best would triumph. Hitler visited the Weimar Nietzsche archives several times, and however violently Nietzsche would have protested (he had specifically denounced nationalism and race hatred fifty years earlier), some of his writings were used effectively by Hitler and others in charge of the ideology of National Socialism.[29] Nietzsche's ideas thus cannot be omitted from an effort to understand the interplay of survival, management and leadership. We will return to him and his influence on Hitler in the next chapter.

Given Nietzsche's intriguing response to Darwin and his uncannily accurate predictions regarding the last century, it is interesting to consider the dim view he took of science in general, and of natural scientists like Darwin in particular. Natural scientists, he said, seemed to be "common people" who had gotten bound up in Darwin's idea, perhaps because their ancestors were "poor and undistinguished people who knew the difficulties of survival" firsthand. "The whole of English Darwinism breathes something like the musty air of English overpopulation, like the smell of the distress and overcrowding of small people."[30] Science was essentially a kind of morality, and was guilty, he said, of the same piety that crippled other forms of morality. It rested on a belief in the need for and superiority of truth; a commitment to seek and discover the truth, and never to deceive anyone, even oneself, in the questions that were asked and the answers that were discovered. Nietzsche was amused by this paradoxical attitude. "Why don't you want to deceive," he asked, if you see no morality in life itself?[31]

Natural Science's Modern World: Nietzschean Darwinism?

Modern natural science has come down on the side of Darwin, implicitly rejecting Nietzsche's view and concluding that natural selection—the struggle for survival—is an adequate paradigm. But in one important respect, though it may not wish to admit the fact, natural science has reached another conclusion that is in complete agreement with him. Like Nietzsche, neo-Darwinian natural science sees life as devoid of an overarching purpose.[32] In a world heavily conditioned by modern technology, the most visible product of our sciences, leaders and managers should pause to give this some thought. Nietzsche reached his conclusions more or less philosophically, but how did science get there?

As noted above, it seems logical to exclude "purpose" from a description of a chemical reaction, or of the way planets move in orbit. Indeed, Isaac Newton, who held to a big picture understanding of the cosmos that depended entirely on purpose, was the first to think in such terms. On the other hand, it seems difficult to fully describe something like human behavior without using the concept of purpose; this Newton did not and would not do. An artist painting a picture can be described in terms of the cause-effect process that begins with an electrical impulse from the brain traveling to the muscles of the hand and arm. Molecules of paint are detached by friction from the brush in the moving hand, adhering to a fibrous substrate (the canvas), and so on. This sort of exhaustive description of a work of art would take a long time and be quite elaborate, but in the end no one would be satisfied that it was complete. So how is that science now claims to eliminate the category of purpose from *any* kind of description? The outcome is of primary concern here, but the process deserves a word or two.

Darwin's methodological forefather was Georges-Louis Leclerc, the Count of Buffon. Born in France in 1707, a large inheritance freed him to pursue his true interest—science. Among his many projects was the development of a natural, as opposed to theological, account for the formation of the earth. He believed that what *is* happening held all necessary clues to what *had* happened and *would* happen. "Events which occur every day, movements which succeed each other and repeat themselves without interruption...those are our causes and our reasons."[33] In short, Buffon believed that cause and effect could explain all natural phenomena, including the age of the world and the adaptations and diversity of living creatures. Although a practicing Catholic, science and theology were parallel faiths for him; he only professed to understand the former.

Newton's approach in the physical sciences and Buffon's in the natural sciences presaged a modern disposition which assumes that purpose, as a category of explanation, has no place in any "scientific" description. Following their examples, scientists then extended them to look for the explanation of all things and all behaviors without reference to purpose. The result is a common modern assumption that everything *can* be understood in terms of cause and effect—even the movements of the artist above. In this scientific world, purpose is a form of speculation, and all forms of speculation are to be replaced by what can be deduced from collections of observable "facts." All of life and the physical world can therefore be understood mechanistically.[34]

Though other branches of science have begun to question the purely mechanistic model, most natural scientists are convinced it is a sufficient and effective means of explaining our world. Some problems with the mechanistic model will be considered briefly in a later chapter, but the point here is to highlight some conclusions of natural science that are relevant to managers and leaders. How do the most famous of these scientists describe the environment in which leaders and managers do their work? Stephen Jay Gould, the world-famous Harvard zoologist, summarizes the natural science perspective this way:

> We are here because one odd group of fishes had a peculiar fin anatomy that could transform into legs for terrestrial creatures; because comets struck the earth and wiped out dinosaurs, thereby giving mammals a chance not otherwise available (so thank your lucky stars in a literal sense); because the earth never froze entirely during an ice age; because a small and tenuous species, arising in Africa a quarter of million years ago, has managed, so far, to survive by hook and by crook. We may yearn for a "higher" answer—but none exists. This explanation, though superficially troubling, if not terrifying, is ultimately liberating and exhilarating.[35]

Renowned British physicist Stephen Hawking's version of the big picture is perhaps less ambiguous than Gould's:

> Yes, man is determined, but since we do not know what has been determined, he may as well not be. One of my biggest concerns for us as human beings is this: natural selection has brought us so far, and we tend to forget that it came about by virtue of natural rejection and aggression. My only hope is that we will keep from eating each other up for another one hundred years, because I am confident within a hundred years

we will find technology able to move us to different planets, and then no one great tragedy or atrocity will devour all of us at the same time.[36]

Hawking made these comments nearly ten years ago; he reiterated them in January of 2001.[37] Faithful to their scientific morality, these respected minds are honest with us about the answers they have found (or not found). They don't attempt to soft-pedal their conclusions so as to make them less disturbing.

Nietzsche, however, might tease them about this, reminding them that, if they really *do* agree with him that there is no higher meaning, they need be so very honest only if doing so aids them in the pursuit of their own personal agendas. Nietzsche's likely response points us directly to the critical implications of the natural science view for managers and leaders.

Concluding Unscientific Postscript

In a mechanistic description of reality, there is no such thing as right or wrong. It is easy to say that the behavior of animals is not immoral; predators are not evil just because they kill and eat their prey. When animals use violence to establish dominance, their behaviors are not "unethical," for the animals are only behaving according to their natures. Natural science, at least in the vision of Gould and Hawking, has no alternative but to view human behavior in the same way, for it simply reports what *is*. Behaviors may be more or less beneficial to the species, but not "good" or "bad" in and of themselves. If there is no overarching purpose or design, our existence is a product of random processes, and our actions are products of physical cause and effect. Our "choices" cannot therefore be described as moral or immoral, even the choices of a Hitler. Rather, they are either more or less advantageous to us individually or to our groups: our countries, communities, organizations or families.

In this scientific perspective, morality relates to values, but values have no referent in reality outside each individual. All that exists arose purely by chance. As Gould puts it,

> [W]ind back life's tape to the dawn of time and let it play again—and you will never get humans a second time. ...We cannot read the meaning of life passively in the facts of nature. We must construct these answers ourselves....[38]

From his view, Nietzsche would tell Gould that he need not be a martyr. He should feel free to "construct those answers" in whatever way best serves Gould and the people or things he cares most about. There is no reason not to.

Leadership and management are both ways of taking action in the world around us. Those actions logically depend on how we perceive that world. The preceding discussion highlighted variations on a common theme in modern perception: the struggle for survival and power. If we accept that theme—that is, if we believe it correctly and sufficiently captures the patterns of human activity—then leadership as a concept cannot in any defensible way be considered distinct from management. We can conclude that none of the larger worlds we have described (Darwinian, Nietzschean, or neo-Darwinian) have room for a category of behavior that can meaningfully be called "leadership."

It is important to concede that some extraordinarily intelligent people have adopted the survival paradigm. But if these individuals are right—if a struggle for survival and power is all there is and all there can be—life is then a problem of management, not leadership. Leaders have nothing to contribute in such a world, because the goal, the means to the goal, and the reason for the goal are already known: the goal is to survive, by all means possible, for no reason at all. No leaders are needed to guide us out of such a forest, for there is no way out.

Leadership bears an essential relation to purpose. In some ultimate sense, it has to do with movement toward a goal, for a reason. Leadership, therefore, is something that *should* be done. There is no "shouldness" in the survival paradigm, for there is no basis for arguing that one *ought* to survive. Though most living things do in fact choose to pursue it, survival in and of itself has no purpose, and doing something that has no purpose can never be meaningfully understood as an authentic form of progress. In the absence of authentic progress or the attempt to make authentic progress, there is no leadership.

3

Managing to Survive

The stern and stony eye of science seeks answers that are not grounded in the fundamentality of purpose.   – Peter Atkins

Humanity is a private feeling, not a public principle to be acted upon.   – The Earl of Abingdon

We are living in a material world.   – Madonna

The Meaning of "Is"

We have all used or heard, probably even in the last week, the common expression, "I'll manage." We also know and often hear the two most common variants of that expression, "I'll get by," and "I'll survive." Sometimes people combine them, as in "I'll manage to get by," or "I'll manage to survive." Language here offers us an important clue regarding the essence of management. For while we can say "I'll manage to survive" and expect to be clearly and correctly understood, the same is not true of the reverse. To say, "I'll survive to manage," or "I'll get by to manage," would have a peculiar, if not incomprehensible, meaning to listeners.

The fact that "I'll manage to survive" is largely redundant while the reverse is almost nonsensical points to two of the foundational assumptions of this book. First, though it can be used in other ways as well, management is often best understood as a means used by individuals and groups to survive or gain additional power. (Used in this sense, power also refers to the resources needed to increase comfort or pleasure.) Second, management tells us nothing about the *purpose* of survival. Management enables us to survive, but cannot tell us why we should do so.

In all cases and contexts, management has to do with what "is," but plays no role in determining what "ought" to be. In many cases, what *is* is the struggle to remain alive or acquire additional resources. Management is then essentially an instinctual, behavioral response to the environment, guided by the assumed imperative of survival. No ethical principles are involved. An executive is one who executes, and "to execute" has two common meanings: one is to carry out instructions or plans, the other is to kill. The objective is predetermined in both cases. Execution is exclusively a question of process.

This is not to malign management as being in any way a negative, unimportant, or necessarily immoral activity. On the contrary, it should be obvious that without management, nothing whatsoever, survival included, is possible. Even a hunger fast requires management (of fluid intake, for example) if it is to last very long. The point that must be grasped about management is that it is a fixture in both kinds of activities and behavioral worlds—those with and those without purpose. Management is *a tool*, and as such it a morally neutral activity. Because management thrives whether or not it is a means to a *purpose*, it is most starkly revealed in worlds without purpose such as the Darwinian, neo-Darwinian, and Nietzschean worlds. In these worlds, there is no problem of distinguishing management from leadership, because leadership, as stated earlier, cannot occur in the absence of purpose. Examining management in such worlds is therefore a helpful step toward separating management from leadership in worlds of purpose.

This chapter, therefore, as a means to briefly analyzing some broad categories of management behavior, does so in the survival context—a context without a transcendent purpose or ethic, characterized by the self-interested behavior of individuals and/or collectives (groups of some sort). Rules or expectations of various kinds operate within the confines of collectives, but these are assumed to have no validity or meaning outside those collectives. Behaviors are evaluated in terms of their usefulness to the individual or collective in the struggle for survival or power, not in terms of moral or ethical principles by which the same behaviors would be evaluated in a world of purpose. Looking at the survival context in terms of Harvard psychologist Lawrence Kohlberg's levels of moral development, the highest level, that of universal principle, does not occur within it. His two lower levels, concern for oneself and for one's group, do.[1]

As noted early in the book, here again we encounter the problem of everyday English lacking the exact terminology needed to quickly make distinctions of type. The names chosen below are probably not familiar ones, at least with respect to characterizations of management, and readers are invited to substitute other names which seem more intuitive if they so desire. Whatever names are used, the three larger worlds considered earlier translate into three broad but unique categories of management behavior. Here, they are referred to as "Darwinian management" (or *scientific management*), "neo-Darwinian supermanagement" (*supermanagement*, for short), and Nietzschean "domination."

Darwinian Management: The Science of Process

This category is the one most familiar to us, the one we usually assume is meant when we hear the word "management" in a business or organizational context. It is a product of science. When survival is assumed to be the dominant priority and only principle underlying practice, scientific management illustrates in stark relief the tool-like nature of all forms of management.

Industrial Taylorism is perhaps the most famous example in this category.[2] Philosopher Mary Midgley notes that Taylorism's shaping of industry to treat all workers, "systematically and on principle," simply as physical components in the manufacturing process, is done without reference to the workers' points of view. Henry Ford was the first to adopt F.W. Taylor's ideas on a large scale. Employees were to be viewed strictly in functional terms. In Ford's words,

> The principal part of a chisel is the cutting edge. ...If there is a single principle on which our business rests, it is that it makes no difference how finely made a chisel is or what splendid steel it has in it...if it has no cutting edge, it is not a chisel. ...The cutting edge of a factory is the man and the machine on the job.[3]

Taylor is seen as the father of scientific management because his essential logical principle, which states that there must be one best way of performing work, has yet to be refuted. If an end product can be specified, there *must* be one best causal sequence of means to that end. Management on this basis can truly be scientific, as quantitative operations such as problem factoring, task analysis, decision science, operations research or time and motion study will ultimately lead to the solution of any production problem.

Pure management puts its "faith" in the "metavalues" of efficiency and effectiveness. The end is never questioned; it is a given. That end is the survival (and growth) of the individual or collective, a goal to be pursued by the most efficient, effective means possible. The focus is on the means to that goal. This spirit of rational enquiry, reinforced by technological advances in the early twentieth century, gave birth to theories of bureaucracy, behaviorism, logical positivism and ultimately general systems theory. Following that came the specific variants of Management by Objectives (MBO), Program Evaluation Review Technique (PERT), and Planning, Programming, Budget Systems (PPBS). Hodgkinson reminds us that these became standard features of the curriculum in schools of management and administration. Such has been the history of the "rational scientific ideology."[4]

Management in this realm implies at least some degree of training or expertise in the use of specialized knowledge. In 1597,

Francis Bacon said simply, "Knowledge is power." More recently, one theorist identified five basic analytical skills which are assumed to make up the essence of administration: (1) analysis of *expertise*: the management of knowledge; (2) analysis of *coalitions*: the management of conflict; (3) analysis of *ambiguity*: the management of goals; (4) analysis of *time*: the management of attention; (5) analysis of *information*: the management of inference. Notably, analysis of value or purpose is not one of the five necessary skills.[5]

"Rational scientific ideology" might seem so cold and mechanistic that it would have little appeal today, but the fundamental "value" equation—the calculation of costs and benefits—yields the type of answer that organizations, as moral primitives, relentlessly rely upon. Interestingly, the language used by Burns to describe his theory of "transactional leadership" does not seem at all out of place here.

> This theory...conceives of leader and follower as exchanging gratifications in a political marketplace. They are bargainers seeking to maximize their political and psychic profits. In this marketplace the bargaining is restricted in scope because the process works only in easily identifiable, calculable, tangible, measurable properties.... Most important, the transactional gratification itself may be a superficial and trivial one.... *Adaptability* is the rule—to the extent that leaders become hardly distinguishable from followers. Relationships are dominated by quick calculations of cost-benefits.[6]

Some students of leadership may think it heretical to suggest that transactional leadership is simply a form of scientific management, but the quote is a reminder that individuals, not just collectives, use the strategies in this category. Individuals survive by *managing* the reality of their environment; indeed, organizations are one resource individuals can make use of in pursuing their *own* survival and power. Organizations that fail to recognize and accept this truth usually fail to survive.

Perhaps little more needs to be said about scientific management except to note that the rationalist ideology is unmatched in its ability to subsume other approaches. Its appetite for quantifiable data is insatiable. The human relations (now human resources) movement arose as an opposing ideology, but ultimately morphed with behaviorism into the business school curricula of MBO, PERT and PPBS noted above.[7] Anything that can be measured, even the most humanistic of modern approaches, can be just as easily co-opted.

Neo-Darwinian Supermanagement: Collective Superstition

In a recent book surveying contemporary issues in leadership, one scholar asserts that the role of leadership "is to manage the values of an organization." Soon thereafter, he asserts additionally that leadership "is about initiating change in an organization."[8] In these two quotes are found the clues to a second important category of management in a world without purpose. *Supermanagers*, for want of a better term, are those individuals who identify, clarify, define, promote, instill or operationalize the values of an organization (a collective) so as to help the organization be more successful in achieving its primary goal: survival. In the words of one such individual, "The challenge is posed by what's out there and by our need to survive."[9]

Although they may resemble them, supermanagers are not leaders. The primary distinction between them has to do with the definition and use of values. For the supermanager, values are a tool used to motivate and unify members of a collective. They comprise an ethical system internal to the collective, and are functional means to an end. The values employed in this way are different from values in larger ethical systems in two important respects: they arise from within the collective, and they have no function or force outside the collective. Values, together with the related idea of "vision," are useful to the supermanager because they are such effective motivators. Not only do they guide action and thinking within the collective, but they also create a heightened sense of identity and belonging among members of the collective. But such values are also "scientific" (as opposed to transcendent) because they arose from *within* the collective in order to *serve* the collective. Because they are scientific, they are manipulable, and skilled supermanagers can modify, replace or prioritize them in the manner that seems to optimize performance.

To be effective, supermanagers must in some sense "believe" in the collective: either that it should survive, or that it should be served. During the workday they are believers, and, for at least as long as they are employed there, they want to influence members of the collective to believe also. They are evangelists. Training programs for supermanagers illustrate the point. A trainer in one such program currently popular in the U.S. states his goal in these terms: "I want customers to be wildly passionate about buying our products, and our employees to be wildly passionate and enthusiastic about making those products." In another program, a slightly less exuberant trainer explains the four elements of "vision": it is developed by those at the top, is shared with and supported by the team, is comprehensive yet specific (detailed), and it is positive and inspiring. Vision gives direction to values, and the end result of vision, says the trainer, is "empowerment."

These examples fail to cut to the heart of the issue, however, for they might appear in similar forms in a world of purpose as well. Ironically, a recent conception of leadership provides exactly the clarification needed. As noted earlier, Joseph Rost's definition of leadership—"an influence relationship between leaders and followers who intend real changes that reflect their mutual purposes"—respects the autonomy and value of the individuals who are in the relationship. Individuals must not sacrifice integrity to be in the relationship; they must freely choose to participate.[10] An organization committed to the dignity of members so interpreted would strive to operationalize this value in all interactions within the organization. Here the distinction between a management value and an ethical value becomes apparent. Rost's value and its operative constraints need *not* apply to individuals who are not members of the organization, such as its customers or neighbors, or to the interactions of members with non-members. It also need not extend to the organization's *means* of pursuing its goal of survival, other than to preclude means which would violate the freedom of choice of its members. The management value of human dignity, it might be said, has limited jurisdiction.

Supermanagers, if they judge it to be an efficient and effective use of value, can make good use of Rost's definition of leadership without violating it in any sense. Hodgkinson notes that the members of an organization "achieve ego-satisfaction to the extent that their values are perceived by them to be taken into the organizational account."[11] Ego-satisfaction translates into better production. The critical point that must be stressed here, however, is that values defined in this way, and the ethical principles which express them, are radically different from ethics and values as understood in a world of purpose. In a world of purpose, and in the most common sense, ethics are universal; their jurisdiction cannot be limited. A person who on the basis of ethical principle sought daily to respect the dignity of his co-workers, for example, would seek to do the same in his interactions with members of his family, or with clerks in the grocery store. If he did not, he would be considered a hypocrite. But there is no hypocrisy in the supermanager's methodology, for the "value" being utilized is of a different ilk. It is a tool, selected for use within clearly defined limits to serve the collective self-interest, as is normal in a world without purpose. Whether or not Rost's definition would legitimize hypocrisy in a world of purpose is an important question that will be considered in a later chapter.

Numerous contemporary conceptions of leadership can be co-opted by supermanagers in a similar manner. Norman Lear, chairman and CEO of ACT III Communications, praised a recent book on leadership for having unembarassingly restored the lofty concepts of "inspiration" and "spirit" to "their rightful place at the core of successful business." Another CEO stated that the authors had "put their words and ideas behind the central issue of competitive business success—leadership!" The book in question, James Kouzes and Barry Posner's popular *The Leadership Challenge*, is not written from the perspective of a purposeless world. The authors believe that the most admired leaders are those who have ethical aspirations and know that "people aspire to live up to the highest moral standards."[12] They assume that the world is one of purpose.

Kouzes and Posner recognize the importance of values such as freedom, community, excellence, service, and social responsibility among others, but they also recognize their utility. "There's rich opportunity for leaders to appeal to more than just…material rewards."[13] They affirm that great leaders create meaning, not just money. Their definition of leadership, however ("the art of mobilizing others to want to struggle for shared aspirations"), could just as easily be used in a world devoid of purpose.[14] This definition is co-opted whenever the meaning created (and made explicit in the form of values and vision) has a strictly organizational referent, arising from within the organization and designed to serve it.

Supermanagers living in a world without purpose are open to anything that improves the bottom line. Burns identifies the "modal values" of honesty, integrity, trustworthiness, and accountability as "crucially important" to transactional leaders, because such leaders depend on partners, competitors and clients "to live up to promises and understandings, as they must themselves."[15] Supermanagers recognize and make use of the logic in that statement. Values are important to collective success, and are carefully evaluated in terms of their capacity to enhance survival.

Under the survival paradigm, political office in a democracy is yet another form of supermanagement. Officeholders in such a context seek to understand and then carry out the wishes of the group, because the group "knows best what it wants *and* what it ought to want."[16] The politician sees herself or himself as an exponent of the group's self-defined ideological agenda and material needs. Determining the predominant consensus within the represented party and then translating that consensus into policy initiatives are paramount concerns. The concerns of those outside the represented party (or state or nation) are heeded only to the extent that their needs or values happen to coincide with those of the represented, or where such heed will translate into advantage for the party in power, such as in improving chances for re-election. This is democracy in its primitive sense. In a world without purpose, only laws and regulations designed to protect those outside the represented party keep it from becoming even more primitive.

In sum, the only "value" which cannot be manipulated by the supermanager is the survival of the collective itself, for it is a constant representing reality. Where the scientific manager has two metavalues, efficiency and effectiveness, the supermanager has one: collective self-interest. The scientific manager is a mathematician; the supermanager is a psychologist.

Nietzsche's Superman - The Will to Dominate

Nietzsche himself might object to any consideration of his thought in relation to either management or leadership, because both of those terms imply some sort of necessary involvement with employees, constituents or followers. For him, the "Single Ones" justified their own existence, answered to no one, and sought no followers.[17] The superman's greatness, as noted earlier, lay in his ability to be lonely, hidden, and a world unto himself. Only if necessary would the superindividuals stoop to impose their wishes on the masses of common people around them. History would produce and be dominated by only a relative few of these persons; their concerns would always be with the greatness of their own art, their own use of creative energy. Those of lesser natures would hardly be noticed as the single ones strove to master "the art of living in victory, heroism, and beauty."[18]

From the other side, it may seem just as odd to students of leadership or management to see Nietzsche's name brought into the discussion. Surely the man who helped fuel German fascism, who said that logic is "the conceptual understandability of existence even for idiots," whose art was so important that it could justify the "luxury of destruction" and senselessness, could have little to offer any rational enterprise!

As will be shown, however, such is not the case. In an otherwise excellent book, Nietzsche has recently been invoked as a guide to ethical decision-making for managers. Joseph Badaracco, a Harvard professor of business management, points to Nietzsche's challenge to "become who you are" as an axiom for managers who are facing difficult ethical decisions. Badaracco's use of the German philosopher's early writing is good as far as it goes. For one who believes the world has purpose, and that ethics has a place in that world, it does take courage to stay true to one's convictions and to face the risk of defining oneself in defining moments. But this is a selective and misleading application of Nietzsche's work, for it lifts the selected passage out of the unique worldview that gave rise to it. According to that worldview, the sort of idealism implicit in attempting to live morally was no less than sickness, a kind of "decadence" that infected society and hindered true artistic achievement.[19]

Nietzsche's world had no purpose. Human behavior, he said, is explained by the will to power—the desire for self-assertion. There is no good or bad; there is only greatness and mediocrity. There is no standard for achievement and there is no punishment or reward; greatness defines its own standards and is its own reward. There is no value in loyalty; greatness must be true only to itself and its own vision. The here and now is all there is; nothing exists after it or above it. These statements describe the world as Nietzsche understood it, but they also represent a piercing critique of modern western culture. An advertising slogan popularized some years ago said, "You only go around once in life, so grab for all the gusto you can get." This, Nietzsche would say, is exactly what mediocrity seeks and is satisfied with. Such small goals result in "a society in which the members continually work hard [to] have more security: and security is now adored as the supreme goddess."[20] Such is the life of animals, too. Greatness demands more.

In the Nietzschean world, the "superindividuals" relevant to this discussion are those who use management exclusively as an avenue to personal validation. In this world, the "great man theory" familiar to students of leadership is more correctly understood as a theory of management. "Great ones" do not seek achievement as a means to service, though service may be a coincidental by-product of their achievement. They seek achievement because it is the only standard by which to measure their lives, and in their view, managerial achievement is defined by the ability to gain and wield increasing amounts of power and influence. This definition necessarily involves others, for it involves some form of domination. It requires subjects, and may require adoration from those subjects. The superman's management metavalue is power; the psychologist has become a conqueror.

Nietzsche would have been extremely frustrated by the co-opting of his thought by Hitler. He would probably be equally frustrated by the comparison here of his view of achievement with those of corporate or political power-brokers. In a world described by the statements in the preceding paragraphs, however, both are viable paths to greatness.

Collectives can be a canvas for the superman's art.[21] The techniques required of the artist were outlined many years ago by Niccolo Machiavelli in his Renaissance classic, *The Prince*. They have been updated most notably for the current discussion in two recent books: Gerald Griffin's *Machiavelli on Management: Playing and Winning the Corporate Power Game*, and Jeffrey Pfeffer's *Managing with Power: Politics and Influence in Organizations*. But the superindividual was recognized as a type even long before Machiavelli. Hodgkinson takes us back millennia, not just centuries, to an ancient Sanskrit guide to success for rulers, the *Arthasastra*.

To function best this 'technology of success' requires strict codes or morality for *others*. The proponent himself is amoral or antimoral. His end is his own political success and every means: deceit, treachery, lies, violence, crime, infinite duplicity are justified simply on the positivist criteria of efficiency and effectiveness. His facade, of course, will reveal none of this. Outwardly he will cultivate the smiling or self-effacing image of the trusted leader—father of his people—a pillar of moral integrity and credible righteousness.... In the extreme, and for him ideal, case, the seeker of success would be the *sole* immoralist—a one-eyed man in a kingdom of the blind...the social conditioning and programming provided by public morality and organizational norms is desirable in that [they render] men predictable and manipulable.[22]

The political usefulness of an emphasis on morality still rings true today, but one might think it dated and irrelevant to super-individuals in the modern corporate world. This would be to miss the point that morality is only a tool. If power and its trappings can instead be gained without morality or even by defying morality, these immediately become attractive options.[23] "Organizational norms" will suffice. Hugh Hefner and Larry Flynt of *Playboy* and *Hustler* magazines illustrate the point, as do Vince McMahon, Jr. and others at the top of professional wrestling. They are the lords of the modern Nietzschean jungle. Everything depends on the particular work of art being created. Reminding us again of the masses' insatiable desire for amusement, Nietzsche would be unsurprised to see his version of greatness expressing itself in the entertainment industry. The World Wrestling Federation would not have fit his personal tastes, but it is domination with *style*, and he was all for that.[24]

In his introduction to *Machiavelli on Management*, Griffin rightly points out that power itself is neither unscrupulous nor compassionate: "it is only power—raw power."[25] He is correct, for like management itself, power is a fixture in worlds with and without purpose alike. His stated purpose in writing is to facilitate compassionate uses of power, he says, because he believes the world should be a more compassionate place. But like Badaracco's use of Nietzsche, Griffin's use of Machiavelli for moral ends is conflicted. Griffin's introduction affirms virtue, but no such affirmation is to be found in the body of his translation of *The Prince* into modern managerial axioms. Pfeffer is more matter-of-fact. In *Managing with Power*, he has nothing to say about morality, ethics, or obligation. "Getting things done" has a strictly organizational meaning; it has to do with the goals of the organization, whether they be good or bad. Success has to do with organizational goal attainment, and in Pfeffer's view, success is achieved only with power. The nature of the goals is simply not part of the question.

Getting things done often requires interaction with others. In the modern world, those "others" are usually members of an organization or a political constituency. Pfeffer ends his book by pointing to Henry Ford II and Lyndon Johnson as skilled users of power. Ford had "the political savvy to get things done, and the willingness to force the issue."[26] Johnson is a more interesting case because, as Pfeffer points out, he seems to have been two different people. The Johnson who in 1948 opposed federal anti-lynching legislation, who in 1968 did not run for re-election largely due to having misled the American people about Vietnam, and who otherwise did "almost nothing to speak out on issues of national importance," was the same person who "almost single-handedly passed more civil rights legislation in less time with greater effect than anyone else in U.S. history."[27] Pfeffer attempts no explanation of LBJ's enigmatic behavior, but the Machiavellian power paradigm fits well. Effective users of power know how to reverse positions if necessary to turn imminent defeat into victory. It is a technique of their art.

Burns offers a more recent example in his study with Georgia Sorenson of the Clinton-Gore administration. Clinton's flirtation with military service in the Vietnam years, Burns says, involved scheming and calculating "on every mile of a tortuous road" to evade both the Reserve Officer Training Corps (ROTC) and the draft, but he still wanted to be seen as a patriot. In Clinton's own words, his goal was to maintain his "political viability within the system." And so he did, by bringing to the issue, as Burns puts it, "all of his qualities except principled conviction."[28]

It can be noted in passing that the "superman" category also opens a fascinating array of new possibilities in the age of globalization and the internet. Journalist Thomas Friedman suggests that a new class of "super-empowered individuals" will arise due to globalization's simultaneous removal of walls that once prevented interaction and its wiring of the entire world into networks. Friedman sees this confluence of circumstance creating an environment that will offer unprecedented opportunity for persons acting alone to influence both markets and nation-states.[29]

Summary

Clues to the nature of pure management can be found in Pfeffer and Griffin's avoidance of the term leadership, and in their almost complete lack of reference to ethics or principle. In the few instances where the words "leader" or "leadership" do occur, they are clearly synonymous with "manager" or "management." No distinction between leadership and management is ever attempted or acknowledged, because in a world without purpose, such distinctions are false. These authors implicitly recognize that where might makes right, there is no purpose, that where there is no purpose, there is no ethics, and where there is no ethics, there is no leadership. But what was said at the outset should be reiterated here. Management in and of itself is in no way a negative, unimportant, or immoral activity. Though it is most starkly outlined in a world without purpose, wherein there is no necessary constraint on how it may be used to exclusively serve individual or collective goals, management is also a necessary element in a radically different conception of reality. In a world of purpose, management is a tool of leadership, and it is to that world we now turn.

Part III

LEADERSHIP AND PURPOSE

The whole future of the sciences is staked on an attempt to understand this canvas and these colors, but not the image...without such a regulative total image they are strings that reach no end anywhere and merely make our lives still more confused....
— Friedrich Nietzsche

4

A World of Purpose

The universe we observe has precisely the properties we should expect if there is at bottom no design, no purpose, no evil, no good, nothing but pointless indifference.
— Richard Dawkins

If I want to be successful I need to have them too—and I do want to be successful, though I don't know at what at the moment. — Jenna Franklin, 15, who asked for breast implants for her 16th birthday

Science and Purpose

Views of famous scientists notwithstanding, the idea of living in a world without purpose troubles many people. Some just aren't very comfortable saying that all behaviors are natural and therefore devoid of any moral content or value, especially if such a view means there is no basis for condemning the actions of a Hitler or a Pol Pot. That our existence is entirely a product of chance, or that our only hope for avoiding complete self-destruction is to somehow populate other worlds—such ideas lead many to think that science has missed something. As one commentator asks, who can live with a theory that tells us that "morality is merely an adaptation put in place to further our reproductive ends"?[1] It turns out that a number of natural scientists aren't very comfortable with the implications of such ideas, either.

Darwin himself struggled with the apparent consequences of his theory. He was torn regarding his concluding remarks in *Origin*. Saying that natural selection worked solely "for the good of each being" and tended to "progress towards perfection," he seemed to imply design, or teleology. But when friend and colleague Asa Gray drew attention to this, Darwin protested that if each change was somehow guided by a predetermined design so as to lead to the correct end, there was no need for his theory at all. "If the right variations occurred and no others," he insisted, "natural selection would be superfluous."[2] For his theory to be relevant, variations had to be undesigned and random. Yet he confessed on several occasions to an "inward conviction" that the universe is not the result of chance after all, but requires an intelligent "Mind," some sort of "First Cause."[3] And years later, when Gray credited him with having restored teleology to natural science, Darwin sincerely thanked him.[4]

Philosopher Peter Singer, a committed utilitarian and one of the best-known modern proponents of the survival paradigm, is not entirely comfortable with it either. In his recent book *A Darwinian Left: Politics, Evolution, and Cooperation*, Singer ultimately admits that he is not satisfied with natural selection because it cannot take us where he believes it should. Something else must take us beyond elements of our evolved nature and "conventional Darwinian constraints" that "act against" the idea of impartial concern for others.[5] But these are odd sentiments, for a purely scientific view of the world provides no basis for saying things aren't the way they *ought* to be, especially given the assumption that what exists is simply a product of chance. Singer struggles with the logical difficulty of building a genuine ethic upon a scientific foundation—a foundation presupposing the absence of purpose.[6]

For many years, a major question in this arena had to do with behavior that seemed not to fit the natural selection paradigm. If survival depended on selfish behavior—looking out for number one—how could altruistic behaviors, such as the elaborate cooperation of social insects, be explained? The answer, kin selection, was not to come until 1964, and William Hamilton, the researcher who proposed it, attained celebrity status for having done so. At Hamilton's funeral in 1999, Oxford biologist Richard Dawkins delivered the eulogy, which was reprinted in the *Times Literary Supplement*. "Those of us who wish we had met Charles Darwin can console ourselves," Dawkins began. "We met W.D. Hamilton."[7] But the past three decades have shown that Hamilton's answers actually raised more difficult questions. Harvard naturalist E.O. Wilson was doused with a jug of ice water by a protester for his view that a more elaborate version of natural selection could explain both human and insect behavior. The problem was that his thinking could be used to justify racism and genocide as well as altruism. Since Hamilton, the sociobiological implications of natural selection have generated tremendous controversy in the scientific community.[8]

Stephen Jay Gould is clear regarding his own position. The idea of a world of purpose is a "false comfort," a sort of emotional crutch that is the result of falsely projected human need to feel important.[9] He may be right, but it is fair to point out that Gould's *conclusion* that purpose does not exist is a product of a methodological framework that *assumes* no place for such a category. This point deserves careful thought. From another angle, proving that something does exist is one thing, but most scientists admit the near impossibility of proving that something does *not* exist. A more logical, more scientifically defensible view is that such ideas arose because of their survival value. In his recent bestseller *Consilience*, Wilson argues that there is "a hereditary selective advantage to membership in a powerful group united by devout belief and purpose." Much if not all such behavior, he writes, "could have arisen by natural selection."[10]

The same is true, however, for all behaviors. In Wilson's world, the belief systems and philosophies that arise in various places or cultures have equal status, because all are a product of natural processes. All have their source in a particular cultural history and milieu. The same is no less true of individual variations, or deviations, from cultural norms. John and Jane Smith may love their neighbors while Bill and Betty Jones may poison theirs, but both orientations are naturally determined products of cause and effect. One or the other may be more advantageous to the species, and given other cultural norms already in place, that will work itself out over time. Neither is "wrong" from a scientific point of view. Both cultural and individual norms are relative, and can only be judged in terms of their long-term utility.

Wilson's position in fact only begs the more compelling questions with which the chapter began. If survival is all there is, and belief in purpose is in fact only a product of natural selection, why should anyone be motivated by this awareness to *continue* behaving as if purpose existed? More simply, if yesterday I believed there was a *reason* to act altruistically, and therefore did seek to act that way, but today I am shown that my belief is false, how should I behave tomorrow? More to the point, why then should I continue sticking my neck out for someone else? The scientific answer has two parts. One is that continuing to be altruistic may, in the long run, improve the species' chances for survival. The other is that there is no reason for the species to survive. In the end, science's answers are still inadequate.

Thirteen decades ago, Nietzsche saw what was coming. "It could be said that only a man who has a firm grasp of the overall picture of life and existence can use the individual sciences without harming himself...."[11] A century after Nietzsche, science has given us the vaccines for smallpox and polio, but it is still unable to tell us why we should use them ourselves, to say nothing of why we should *share* them.

The Will to Meaning

It may be, however, that too much has been said here. The choice of whether or not to recognize a world of meaning and purpose is many-faceted and intensely individual. It is perhaps the most fundamental choice facing each one of us, for, varying according to the level of commitment with which that choice is made, it affects in a profound way all that we do and all that we are. This book, as is probably already apparent, assumes that recognizing purpose is the better choice. But, as has been noted, some extremely intelligent people have come down on the other side of the issue. It is fair, though, to point out not only that there are respected scientists who do recognize purpose, but also that those who do not have struggled with the implications of their position.

The next topic to consider here might logically be a review of the fact-value distinction, and of the corresponding naturalistic fallacy—the fallacy of deciding what ought to be on the basis of what is—so important in philosophical debate. Fortunately for the reader, such a review, though relevant, is beyond the scope of this book. It suffices to say that the whole problem boils down to the question of meaning.

If there is meaning in life, there is also purpose. Where purpose and meaning exist, there is also a basis for values, and a justification for ethics. Apart from meaning, ethics is in effect little more than a set of game rules, and game rules can be broken with impunity when no one is looking or when doing so improves the cost-benefit calculus. *Apart from meaning, ethics has no motive force.* And ethics, it is argued here, is the foundation of leadership. Having noted the moral dilemmas created by the survival paradigm, nothing further will be said to defend the assumption that our lives do have meaning. Yet it is important to be clear about "the meaning of meaning" as it is used here.

The most influential recent thinker on this subject is Viktor Frankl, the famous psychiatrist and concentration camp survivor who founded the logotherapy school of analysis. Frankl sees the human need for direction as one of the keys to meaning. For him, direction is a tension between what one is and what one ought to be, or between what one is doing and what one ought to be doing. Tension is thus a healthy thing when it is aroused by a meaning to fulfill. Freedom by itself is a negative concept that requires the positive complement of "responsibleness." Responsibleness has two referents, Frankl says: it refers to a meaning we are responsible to fulfill, and to some sort of entity to which we are responsible. But meaning is also relative to some degree because it is "related to a specific person who is entangled in a specific situation," and life itself "is a string of unique situations."[12]

Frankl's position on meaning is controversial because it challenges a number of modern tendencies. Although relative in the sense just explained, meaning for Frankl is not something we can create for ourselves. Whatever is true and real has been so for a long time. In his book *The Will to Meaning*,[13] Frankl argues persuasively that true meaning is something outside, something we did not create and toward which we can move. Self-created meaning has no anchor; it is akin to throwing a rope into the air and then trying to climb it. Likewise, self-created meanings demand neither accountability nor genuine commitment. If I alone create the meaning, how faithful I am to it is no one's business but my own. What human beings truly want, however, are meanings "which are something other than themselves...more than mere projections of these selves. Meanings [that] are discovered but not invented."[14]

Frankl does not tell us what meanings he believes honest seekers will find. His point is that independent, self-created meaning is immediately confronted on all sides by other self-created meanings that demand equal legitimacy. As the sociobiology controversy above illustrates, there is no larger authority to appeal to when one meaning, seeking its own fulfillment, transgresses the space of another. As another writer puts it, casually composing a "personal collage" of meaning using "spare parts" from various belief systems is highly presumptuous.[15] Thus, the search for meaning must itself be an act of "responsibleness." It must involve genuine looking, as through a telescope to things outside the self, rather than as into a kaleidoscope at only what is inside the self. Not just any answer will do, for we are to seek right answers, and true meaning.

Meaning, once found, deposits purpose squarely in our path. Centuries ago, Frankl says, the Jewish sage Hillel framed the situation best. "If I don't do it—who will do it? And if I don't do it right now—when should I do it? But if I do it for my own sake only—what am I?"[16]

Frankl once observed that Americans obsessively avoided coming across as authoritarian, or as even mildly directive, perhaps because of an internalized reaction against the authoritarian nature of Puritan morality. The converse was also apparent: Americans seemed to have a collective fear that meaning and purpose might be imposed upon *them*, and so tended to avoid discussion of such topics. But Hillel's questions seem to go straight to the heart of this matter of leadership. Somehow, in the age of science, much that is written about leadership "manages" to avoid discussion of larger purposes.

If there really is such a thing as a world of purpose, what is it like? Two characteristics provide the boundaries for a theory of leadership grounded in ethics. First, in such a world, assumptions about what is *good* are different. Second, in a world of purpose, the concept of *success* takes on a radically different meaning.

The Good is Common

In a world of purpose, a working notion of "the good" is the most important, yet most elusive, concept of all. Theologians and philosophers have studied, debated and struggled with the specifics for thousands of years; we will certainly not resolve here all of the issues involved. There are two points that can be reasonably asserted, however, and they provide a starting point for any discussion related to ethics. The first point is that, in a world of purpose, there *is* something called the good, and it is defined by the purpose and meaning of our lives. Our search for meaning will lead us toward an understanding of "the good."

The second point is that the overall meaning of the good does not vary from place to place, from time to time, or from person to person. Ethical principles, as noted earlier, are universals, because the notion of the good supporting each ethical system is also assumed to apply universally. Ethical principles stemming from the recognition of human dignity, for example, are understood to apply to all people, not just some. How we understand the good will vary according to the fruits of our search for meaning (described above by Frankl), but genuine sources of meaning will always assume a definition or source of the good, and will make that good universally applicable. Ethical systems differ, but all agree that what is good is common.

The next logical question may well be, "So?" All of this may be true, but what is its practical utility? We want and need specifics, but the common good is not easy to define. It is in some ways easier to offer concrete examples, as in this excerpt from a university chancellor's address to students at the beginning of a recent school year.

> We hope four years from now, when you graduate, you will feel prepared to create [a] better world. It would even be okay if you got started before you graduated. What do we mean by "a better world"? I don't know. It seems like it wouldn't be a bad idea if the world was a place where children didn't go hungry, where disease is cured, where respect for others is a way of life, where we recognize there are spiritual forces larger than ourselves, and where both the mind and body are developed to their full potential. I don't know if that would be a better world or not, but it seems like it would be a good start....[17]

In their book *Leadership for the Common Good*, John Bryson and Barbara Crosby take a similar approach, suggesting in general but practical terms what serving the common good might mean. Despite the title of their book, they never attempt to directly define the concept itself. Readers can infer, however, that Bryson and Crosby understand the common good to involve "mutual gain that serve[s] people's deepest interests in safety, justice, economic well-being, environmental saneness, liberty, and community." It involves "discovering possibilities for joint gain and avoiding the likelihood of mutual loss."[18]

The speech and book both offer helpful specifics. Most ethical systems, if not all, will affirm those examples of serving the common good. Both imply that some ways of acting are expressions of the good while others are not. But given the need for a concept clear enough to incorporate into a theory of leadership, can we not do more than simply list a few general examples and broadly-stated end values? We can indeed, but maybe only a *little* more.

Though it may seem to be a stating of the obvious, the most important point to be made about the common good is that it is not the same as the collective good. What an individual sees as "good," in the sense that it is in his or her own best interest, may or may not serve the interests of a collective of which he or she is a member, and vice versa. What is "good" for a collective—a family, an organization, a community, a corporation, a nation—may or may not be "good" for those who are outside the collective, and vice versa.

For our purposes in this chapter, the latter distinction is the important one. It can be seen in four scenarios that may occur in the interaction of a collective with the rest of society. In the first, what serves the collective good also serves the larger common good. In the second, the relation is neutral; that is, what is good for the collective has no appreciable effect on those outside the collective. In the third, what is good for the collective is bad for others, or, conversely, what serves the common good does not serve the collective. In the fourth scenario, what is good for the collective negatively affects an individual member of the collective such that the larger common good also suffers. For example, a company may improve efficiency by transferring an employee to another city, but if the employee's family is harmed as a result, both the family and society at large are negatively impacted. In sum, the common good and the collective good may or may not be congruent.

Much more can and should be said about the common good. The brief sketch above only scratches the surface of a large, complex concept, but it is offered merely as a starting point. The same is true of the definition below. Consistent with the purposes of this book, a broad working definition is offered as a point of departure for further discussion and debate. Borrowing some language from Bryson and Crosby, the common good may be defined as *that which serves the deepest interests of all people involved*. This definition will be incomplete or unsatisfactory for some, but it can serve as a starting point.[19]

Before moving on, it should be noted that Bryson and Crosby (without intending to do so) raise an interesting question. Their book centers on a category of leadership they call "public leadership." Public leaders are those who attempt to inspire and mobilize others to work together "to resolve important public problems effectively and ethically, thereby contributing to the common good. Public leadership stimulates vision, hope, courage, and commitment."[20] There is much to be commended here, but the authors imply that public leadership is a type specifically concerned with the common good. By extension, other types of leadership may have different concerns. But if public leaders are the ones concerned with the common good, is that sort of concern merely optional for other kinds of leaders? Do other kinds of leaders serve various collective goods without respect to the common good?

We will return to this pivotal issue in the next chapter, but pointing it out here serves two purposes. First, it draws attention to the difference between the collective good and the common good. This important conceptual distinction, if mentioned at all, is often blurred in contemporary writing about leadership. For example, two articles in Ciulla's *Ethics, The Heart of Leadership*, despite purportedly being concerned with this very problem, overlook the need to define basic terms. Both writers, Michael Keeley and J. Thomas Wren, cast the common good question in terms of the tension between individual and group interests, or between smaller group (factional) and larger group interests. In so doing, they confuse the distinction between group good and a larger good. The confusion is obvious in this excerpt from Wren's discussion of the "common good" in the writings of an American founding father. Interestingly, the excerpt suggests a similar lack of clarity in the writing of both Burns and leadership theorist Bernard Bass.

> Burns makes the point strongly: "leadership is nothing if not linked to *collective* purpose." Similarly, Bass notes that "transformational leadership...occurs when...employees...look beyond their own self-interest for the good of the group." That commitment to the *common* good links both formulations to the thought of James Madison.[21] (italics added)

Some will assert that the difference is insignificant, but that assertion cannot be properly debated without some agreement as to the meaning of terms. Herein the terms *collective* and *common* refer to two entirely different things, whether used in conjunction with "the good" or some other aspect of management or leadership activity.

A second point to be drawn from the Bryson and Crosby question is that it helps to illustrate in a slightly different way one of the fundamental differences between a world of purpose and one without. In the survival paradigm, there are only two kinds of "good," one that serves the interests of individuals, and one that serves the interests of collectives. The collective good equates exactly with whatever is most likely to serve the long-term viability of the particular group in question. "Public leaders" in such a world would in fact only be able to serve as brokers representing the interests of one or more collectives. That is, they would be limited to a transactional form of leadership (to use Burns's terminology) serving some form of the collective good. In a world of purpose, that sort of good will not always conform to the common good constraint. "Common good" is an oxymoron in a world without purpose. The idea of the common good complicates things considerably, but it also makes a world of difference.

Success Re-visioned

As part of a homework assignment, a college professor once asked his students to each think of one individual they viewed as successful, and to come to the next class session prepared to tell why they chose whom they did. As it turned out, every member of the class selected a person that was familiar to most or all of their classmates. Andy Grove, Bill Gates, John F. Kennedy, Dwight Eisenhower, Barbara Streisand and Walt Disney were representative of the list of "successful people" the class came up with. When asked to identify characteristics common to everyone on the list, the class noted that each had achieved some sort of public notoriety, and in most cases, significant financial gain as well. When asked to define success in general terms, they ultimately decided, after much discussion, that it boiled down to achieving goals. Successful people were those who set big goals and achieved them.

The students' take on success makes sense. In many ways, success seems to logically equate with achievement. But does this equation work generally? Must a person achieve goals in order to be successful? And, are all who achieve goals judged successful in the end? A famous author once said that he wished he had known earlier in life what he discovered at the high point of his career: "When you get to the top, there's nothing there." This person, for one, would answer the latter question in the negative. Goal achievement, for him, did not equate to success. Martin Luther King was assassinated at the age of 39, and had spoken the day before his death of important things that had yet to be accomplished in the struggle for civil rights. He did not live to see those goals realized, but history has pronounced him anything but a failure. Other examples are close at hand. If a scientist fails after many years of research to discover a cure for cancer, should she be considered a failure? Clearly not, for her work will have served to draw other researchers closer to that cure.

In a world of purpose, the equating of success with attaining goals is called into question. In such a world, success for an individual hinges on something different. Goals themselves are judged by how well they fit into a larger purpose, or, to use the terminology above, by their congruence with the common good. Right goals, assuming that they are vigorously pursued, are the determinants of success. Wrong goals, whether achieved or not, equate to failure.

There is another critical point to be made here. If behavior in a world of purpose is to be guided by an ethical system, then goals must be pursued in an ethical manner. This means that for a person to truly be considered a success, she or he must be able to look back at the end, either of a project or a life, and answer only two questions in the affirmative. First, were the right goals chosen? Second, were they pursued in an ethical manner? The matter of goal attainment is subordinate to other considerations.

This approach to success raises some perplexing issues, however. What if the *wrong* goals are pursued *ethically*, or conversely, the *right* goals are pursued *unethically*? Would those be cases of success, failure, or something else? This is a monumental question. Burns sees the tension "between *modal values* such as fair play...and *end values* such as equality" as the most disruptive force in competitive politics. He could have gone further and identified it as the central test of great leadership.[22] In fact, he almost does.

> It is the lack of modal values—the inhumanity and irresponsibility with which the struggle is conducted—that produces fear and counterrevolution. The American revolution left few deep scars because of the essential fidelity and even civility of revolutionary leaders like Washington and Adams.[23]

Burns is close to answering our "monumental" question. At the very least, success in general is severely compromised—it is *scarred*—if attained by unethical means. Much more could be said here, but for the purposes of this book, the implications of viewing success in this way will be explored in conjunction with the philosophy of leadership developed in the next section.

The "success question" points us directly back to the matter of ethics. Most adults spend the majority of their waking hours at work or thinking about work. Some companies are more able than others to define their corporate purpose in terms of directly and significantly serving the common good because their product or service meets felt needs. Drawing employees into conscious awareness of and participation in this mode of service can justify and add meaning to the significant portion of their lives they devote to an employer. Nearly 50 years ago, an executive named Abram Collier reflected on this aspect of working.

> Business does not exist merely to produce more goods and services, or better goods and services for more people, though that is no small part of its task. [It also] affords the principal or the only means whereby individual men and women may gain the satisfaction of accomplishing *something more than merely sustaining their own lives*.[24] (italics added)

Collier was largely right. He was absolutely right in suggesting that true humanity has to do with something more than mere survival. But there are many paths to meaning in addition to business, and not all businesses or business models can fulfill the role Collier has given them. Individual employees must evaluate what an employer is doing, and how the employer is doing it, in light of the ethical constraints and imperatives that flow from the meaning and purpose they have individually found for their lives. In some cases, they will not be able to participate in good conscience.[25]

Often, however, at least as far as our vocations go, the life purpose we embrace must be expressed more in *how we live* than in *what we do*, either because we do not have high positions or because our jobs are neither unethical nor especially humanitarian. Most people are engaged in something less than leading a country or a charitable organization. The average person does not work where they do because their employer serves some grand and noble purpose for bettering the lot of all humankind. Often their position is simply the best one they could get in a certain location at a certain time.

Individual success in such cases can then be evaluated in terms of questions such as, "Am I working for an employer that, at the very least, is not doing harm to the common good?" and, "How am I making use of discretionary resources, such as my time and money?" and, "Do I live my life ethically, both at work and outside of work?" If true purpose is found, the final evaluation of our lives hinges on our faithfulness to the ethical or moral obligations that follow from that purpose. The question of "right goals" will, for many people, be secondary to the question of "living rightly." That is one way to put it. Another is just to put the two together. Given a job that doesn't harm but also doesn't directly serve the common good, our goal would be to live our daily lives in accordance with the meaning we have found. Our goal would be to live rightly.

It may have only been coincidence that the students mentioned earlier all chose well-known figures as their example of success, but the view of success proposed here is clearly not restricted to the rich and famous. Ordinary people can be successful too. An informal class survey may not be indicative of overall cultural tendencies, but if a society assumes this is not so—if it assumes that success is not something for ordinary people—the consequences cannot be good. Each of us should be able to look around in our circle of relatives, friends and acquaintances and identify one or more who have never graced a magazine cover or had a television feature done on them, yet are successful people in the deepest sense of the word. They should come to our minds when someone asks *us* for success stories.

None of the foregoing is intended to gloss over the question of effectiveness. Very often, goals are not reached simply because the diligence, planning or wisdom needed to achieve them was lacking. But we must sharply distinguish effectiveness from success. One need not attain goals to be successful, especially if the pursuit is ethical. In the survival paradigm, modern success, measured as it is by accumulation, image, amusement and financial security, is radically different from success in a world of purpose. The latter is wholly non-material and guided by meaning; the former is quantifiable and constrained only by tradition (habit) or game rules, neither of which is binding. The two kinds of success are not the same.

Much of what has been said about success can also be said about leadership. One need not achieve goals in order to lead, but the right goals are essential. And one need not be rich, famous, or powerful. Ordinary people can lead, too.

5

Leadership: ~~Survival~~ Service of the ~~Fittest~~ Faithful

I try to get there, and I figure if I do, then other kids might say they're willing to try and go, too, and pretty soon, it could be better for us here."
 — Ruby Bridges, age six, on attending a previously all-white school in the face of an angry mob (early 1960s)[1]

If you're going to lead, you have to win people over to what you believe is the truth, the way to truth, and that means they're willing to put their trust in you, and that's a gift, you know—the leader is given trust because the ones [being led], they believe it's right to follow, right for them and right for what they think is right. — one of Ruby's elementary school teachers[2]

Back to Basics

In the first chapter of this book, the statement was made that leadership, in general terms, is best understood as one way of living an ethical life. Subsequent chapters argued that leadership, as a result, necessarily exists only in a world of purpose and meaning. Purpose provides a touchstone for genuine progress. Leadership, because it is subsumed and bounded by ethics, represents the pursuit of the common good, not just the good of a given collective. Ethics is based upon universally applicable guiding principles, and these constrain both the goals and the means of that pursuit. Management, on the other hand, exists whether or not the world is one of purpose and meaning. In the context of purpose, management is a morally neutral adjunct to leadership. Outside such a context, it stands alone in a moral vacuum as a means to survival or power. The thesis of this book is that management has to do with survival, but leadership has to do with service.

Conceptualizing leadership in this way may seem somewhat idealistic, but the basic idea is not new. For many centuries before the modern age, leaders were much more than managers. In fact, management as it is now understood—the science of specifying means to ends—is the new kid on the block. Leadership theorist Gilbert Fairholm notes that prior to modernity, the great people in society were not just the strongest, the smartest, or those who controlled resources. Chiefs, priests and kings also served as a window or channel to larger reality. "They claimed to have the ear of the gods, receiving inspiration and visions from above."[3] It was their responsibility, their necessary role, to give sense to life.

That is not what is being proposed here. We are fortunate to have moved to the point where average people have some freedom to look elsewhere for "inspiration and visions" if they choose. On the other hand, it would be naïve, and we *have been* naïve, to assume that this freedom grants those in positions of power and authority a correlative freedom to live irresponsibly. We have also been naïve to assume that we don't *need* them to live responsibly. The influence, positive or negative, that persons in authority inevitably exert is again becoming clear. For many reasons, we need that influence to be positive.

The theory of leadership presented here does not contradict other current scholarship. It logically synthesizes and distills much of what is now being written on the subject. Today's most respected theorists are quietly pointing us back to an understanding of leadership interestingly similar to the ancient one that long predated the age of management.

The servant-leader *is* servant first.... That person is sharply different from one who is leader first, perhaps because of the need to assuage an unusual power drive or to acquire material possessions.... The difference manifests itself in the care taken by the servant-first to make sure that other people's highest priority needs are being served.... Do those served grow as persons? Do they, *while being served*, become healthier, wiser, freer, more autonomous, more likely themselves to become servants? *And*, what is the effect on the least privileged in society; will they benefit, or, at least, not be further deprived?
– Robert Greenleaf[4] (italics in original)

Only with time, determination, conviction, and skill...can followers be drawn out of these narrower collectivities and into "higher" purpose and principle validated by the most enduring criteria of justice and humanity and forged in an open and continuing conflict of values.... To define leadership in terms of motivation, value, and purpose is to glimpse its central role in the processes of historical causation. – J.M. Burns[5]

[T]ransforming leadership ultimately becomes *moral* in that it raises the level of human conduct and ethical aspiration of both leader and led.... – J.M. Burns[6] (italics in original)

If we look at the array of societies described by historians and anthropologists, we cannot find an instance of a healthy society in which humans have not devised a framework of values.... We must hope, too, that our leaders will help us keep alive values that are not so easy to embed in laws....
– John Gardner[7]

Pluralism that reflects no commitments whatever to the common good is pluralism gone berserk.... [S]ometimes when each member of a community acts to maximize his or her short-term self-interest, the long-term consequences may be the destruction of values or purposes that the group held in common and did not...wish to destroy. – John Gardner[8]

[M]ost human beings...crave an explicit statement of value—a perspective on what counts as being true, beautiful, and good. [People pay special heed] to those who can provide some kind of broad orientation, if not definitive answers, to essential questions: the purpose of work, the value of prayer, the just distribution of rewards and punishment, and the stance to assume in the face of death and other ultimate human concerns.   – Howard Gardner[9]

[L]eaders serve [humankind] through Meaning. ... [A system of belief] is nothing but marks on paper or vibrations in the air unless and until it roots itself in the values of a man and changes his life. It is the singular wonder of leadership that such a change in one man's life has the potential for changing other lives. ... There is a moral order in the universe; adherence to it strengthens, departure from it weakens [the leader].
                                            – Christopher Hodgkinson[10]

[R]esponsibility must be the principle which informs and organizes the post-capitalist society. The society of organizations, the knowledge society, demands *a responsibility-based organization*.... Organizations have to take "social responsibility." There is no one else around in the society of organizations to take care of society itself. ...An organization has full responsibility for its impact on community and society.... [Organizations have] a responsibility to find an approach to basic social problems that [matches] their competence....   – Peter Drucker[11] (italics in original)

There is a great deal of talk today about "entitlement" and "empowerment." These terms express the demise of the command and control-based organization. But they are just as much terms of power and rank as the old terms were. We should instead be talking about responsibility and contribution. For power without responsibility is not power at all; it is irresponsibility. Our aim should be to make people more responsible.   – Peter Drucker[12]

Great leaders...create meaning, not just money.... There is a deep human yearning to make a difference. We want to know that we've done something on this earth, that our life means something. We want to know that there's a purpose to our existence.... The most admired leaders speak unhesitatingly and proudly of mutual ethical aspirations.
— Kouzes & Posner[13]

For Burns, by definition, the transforming leader was morally uplifting. [I *once* argued] that transformational leaders could wear the black hats of villains or the white hats of heroes depending on their values. (Those who wear black hats [*I now see*] as pseudotransformational.)
— Bernard Bass[14] (italics added)

[Leaders] help shape us morally [and] spur us on to purposeful action..."
— Robert Coles[15]

Leadership...is a complex moral relationship between people, based on trust, obligation, commitment, emotion, and a shared vision of the good. Ethics, then, lies at the very heart of leadership.
— Joanne Ciulla[16]

There are even more, but these serve to make the point: this is not a new idea. The threads of meaning, purpose, and morality run through all of these conceptions. Such is the direction modern scholars are moving as they attempt to grasp the nature of leadership. Ciulla's earlier observation is accurate: *most* scholars and practitioners who write about leadership claim that ethics is important. What has been lacking so far is a distillation of this persistent undercurrent of meaning and value into a basic definition of leadership, rather than into various "types" of leadership. We now read of servant, transformational, transactional, pseudo-transformational, values, ethical, unethical, moral, organizational, and even more "types" of leadership. The basic idea or phenomenon has been layered over with a multiplicity of variants that all seem to be trying to make up for something that was missing in the first place. Everyone keeps going back to the moral-ethical dimension identified by Burns in his original description of transforming leadership. There is a reason for that. When carefully considered, *the leadership concept itself loses significance without ethics.* All roads lead back there.

We will return to some of the reasoning behind that last statement in a moment, but must first turn to Joseph Rost. Rost's important work may be part of the reason why scholars have not tried harder to link ethics and leadership generally. Rost is the notable absentee from the honor roll of leadership theorists quoted above; he is strongly opposed to such ideas.

In his influential 1990 book *Leadership for the Twenty-First Century*, Rost states his position flatly: leadership does not depend on ethics, and because of this we "can expect to see leaders and followers using ethical process to pursue unethical changes, and...using unethical processes to support ethical changes."[17] Rost focuses an entire chapter in his book on the relationship of leadership to ethics. He concludes by saying that although leaders "have the responsibility and the duty to make ethical judgments concerning the changes they intend," the ethical systems available to us create as many problems as they solve. "Our moral systems of thought [and] our moral language, do not encompass a concept of a social vision, a common good, a public interest," and are therefore "inadequate" for making moral judgments about the content of leadership.[18] Only when we have a "new language of ethics" centered on "an integrated concept of the common good" will leaders and followers be able to "make some moral sense" out of the changes they propose.[19] This, he concludes, is because people just have too many different ideas regarding the nature of the good.

This is a curious conclusion in light of some well-known figures in history. Are we really to believe that Abraham Lincoln, Martin Luther King, Nelson Mandela and all of their followers never truly made "moral sense" of the changes they pursued? Rost's position is simply untenable. Leaders make moral sense out of their public lives because they have first made moral sense out of their individual lives; that moral sense is what compels their public activity. This is not to deny the difficulty of their (or anyone's) individual quests for meaning, or to deny the thorniness of the common good issue. But these are hardly excuses for denying the legitimacy and power of lives committed to particular visions of the good. As theologians and philosophers agree, the supreme ethical demands of a given belief system cannot be replaced by a global ideology or by some kind of ethical minimalism.[20] If leaders do not help others make moral sense of the world, how are their activities in any way significantly different from the activities of managers?

This is an extremely problematic aspect of Rost's argument, but it may not be the *most* problematic one. As noted earlier, Rost builds his understanding of leadership on the ethicality of the leader-follower relation. In his words, "The ethics of the leadership process requires that the leaders and followers use influence in their interactions to achieve this mutuality" without violating "the autonomy and value of the individuals who are in the relationship."[21] Without ethics, then, leadership is impossible.

Ethicists must raise strong objections here, for an ethical principle that is practiced in one setting but not another is something less than an ethical principle: it is a game rule, or a term of a contract. Those who might be impacted negatively *by* the collaborative activity—that is, stakeholders outside the relation whose autonomy and value were *not* respected—will not be impressed to learn that the leaders and followers all acted voluntarily.

Rost's theory also has important implications for the integrity of leaders in the eyes of followers, and vice versa. If the leader, for example, proclaims that human autonomy is a critical value in the development of mutual purposes, but then does not apply this value in other settings, his or her credibility will inevitably suffer. Similarly, employees will be less inclined to trust a boss's word in the workplace, no matter how much he stresses the importance of honesty, if they know that he cheats on his taxes or his wife. As one sage put it, a person who is nice to you but rude to the waiter is not a nice person. We will return to this point later.

Having noted these problems, however, it is fully affirmed that the one ethical principle Rost does require is also absolutely essential to the understanding of leadership proposed here. His argument that it must be included in definitions of leadership has stood up well as scholars have analyzed that proposition over the past ten years. They agree that something other than leadership is happening if persons are coerced or manipulated into (or during) the relationship. Rost's identification of the essentiality of this ethical principle is one part of the picture, and is a clue to the larger nature of the leadership phenomenon. We can now assert with a degree of certainty that without some ethical element, leadership does not occur at all.

But one such principle alone, especially when confined to one relation alone, is insufficient. Indeed, an ethical principle so isolated is a contradiction in terms. Leadership theorist Al Gini correctly characterizes ethics as springing from "the will to believe" that "individuals possess certain basic rights that cannot and should not be willfully disregarded or overridden by others." This belief, if adopted, *must* then become a "factual baseline of our thought process for all considerations in regard to others." Ethical behavior and ethical systems in general thus intend no harm, and respect the rights *of all affected*.[22] What leadership scholars have failed to do thus far is to come to grips with the implications of the universality of ethics. By definition, ethics has to do with nothing less than the common good. Once we open the door to one ethical principle, all of its kin—those that together with it make up an entire ethical system—come piling in as well.

What is confusing in current writing is that references to the *common* good, such as those above from Burns and others, usually occur in passing, in the context of discussions focusing on *collective* good situations. For example, Kouzes and Posner's excellent statement quoted above was drawn from their sizable book designed to serve as a handbook for the organizational leader.

Yet, their general definition of leadership in that same book (quoted just below) is much like similar general definitions from other writers in that it is cast in terms that are either explicitly collective- (group- or organization-) oriented or can be freely interpreted to have no referent beyond the collective.

> [W]e define leadership as the art of mobilizing others to want to struggle for shared aspirations. — Kouzes & Posner[23]

> [T]he real role of [leadership] is to manage the values of an organization. — Peters & Waterman[24]

> [Leadership is] the process of followers and the leader engaging in reciprocal influence to achieve a shared purpose. — Rosenbach & Taylor[25]

> Leadership is the process of persuasion or example by which an individual [or team] induces a group to pursue objectives held by the leader or shared by the leader and...followers. — John Gardner[26]

> Leadership is a power- and value-laden relationship between leaders and followers/constituents who intend real changes(s) that reflect their mutual purpose(s) and goal(s). — Al Gini[27]

> [Leadership is] the art of influencing people to accomplish organizational goals...a special technique, a technology, that managers can use to add a substantively new element to their behavior. — Gilbert Fairholm[28]

As the foregoing chapters have attempted to show, however, any sort of activity that focuses only on the betterment of an individual or collective fits nicely into the survival paradigm—a world devoid of meaning and therefore devoid of meaningful ethical systems. Leadership understood only in collective terms cannot be distinguished from management. We cannot give ethics its due in a limited context.

Rost locates the origin of leadership studies as an academic discipline in social psychology, organizational behavior, and political science. Approaching the problem from a social science perspective, he seeks an empirical definition of leadership. On this basis he rejects a moral requirement as to the content (goals) of leadership as "scientifically impossible to accept," because it would be "impossible for analysts to agree on what leadership is, since that is dependent upon what they believe is moral."[29] What he does not admit, however, is that such an approach also precludes his own requirement that the leadership relation be "an ethical one." Against that requirement the very same objections may be raised. Is it not also *scientifically* impossible for analysts to agree on what is an "ethical" relation? The ethical principle of respect for autonomy is grounded in a valuing of human dignity, but values cannot be described or prescribed scientifically. As one scholar puts it, values "do not exist in the world. They are utterly phenomenological, subjective, facts of the inner and personal experience, ultimately only susceptible of location [within the] further and deeper mystery of consciousness...."[30] Scientifically speaking, how would we *know* that the requisite value was present?

But Rost, like Burns, has pointed us in the right direction. Inevitably, leadership must described in value terms, for it resides within the province of ethics. What was said at the outset can now be repeated: if ethics has to do with the common good, and if leadership cannot be exercised apart from ethics, then leadership can also not be divorced from the common good. Leadership is then best understood as one way of living an ethical life; it is ethics involving others in certain relational ways. It is a form of ethical expression, ethical living writ large. As a category, leadership is subsumed within ethics. Rather than in the social sciences, leadership is best understood and located within philosophy. Given this, leadership might then be defined along these lines: *it is the art of guiding followers in collaborative pursuit of a mutually understood aspect of the common good*. According to this definition, ethics constrains both the means and the ends of leadership.[31]

Clarifications and Implications

Such an understanding of leadership depends, first of all, upon the particular notion of *progress* developed in the preceding chapters. That is, genuine progress has to do with movement toward a goal, *and for a reason*. Because there is no "ought," no *reason*, in the survival paradigm, there is no basis for accepting mere survival or acquisition of power as a form of progress.[32] As was argued earlier, though most living things do in fact choose to pursue it, survival alone has no purpose. Doing what has no purpose can never be meaningfully understood as an authentic form of progress.

Applying this perspective to organizations or other collectives, the same conclusion holds: neither their survival nor their flourishing can automatically be equated with progress. Strictly evaluated, the mere pursuit and achievement of collective goals does not equate to authentic progress. Authentic progress occurs only when goals and behaviors serve the common good. Leadership cannot be meaningfully distinguished from management unless linked to some defensible notion of progress. In the cases of Hitler and—as far as anyone can know—Jim Jones and the Jonestown suicides, something other than leadership took place. Authentic progress was not the goal or the result in either case. The same conclusion can be reached from a business perspective. As Drucker puts it, "Without responsibility, power... always degenerates into non-performance."[33]

Purpose, implied in the definition of leadership above by its recognition of a common good, encompasses both ends and means. The pursuit of justice, for example, must itself be characterized by justice. Ends must be lived as well as pursued, and they *cannot* be divorced from one another. That is to say, leadership involves guiding followers in living ethically in two ways. First, to act ethically by pursuing collective goals that *either serve or do not violate* the common good, and second, to act ethically *both within and outside* the collective. Ethical principles are reduced to game rules if limited to interactions with other members of the collective. Genuine ethics cannot be donned at the beginning of the workday and doffed on the way out the door. This is a critical principle to grasp, for it makes leadership accessible to all persons. Even at the very lowest levels of an organization, individual ethical behaviors, if genuine, are themselves an expression of a common good. Such expressions, because they are by definition grounded in purpose, can influence others to join in collaborative expressions of that purpose. The inextricability of means from ends in a world of purpose carries additional implications that will considered later.

Leadership is necessarily relational, but it is also intensely personal. Leaders and followers, who always begin in some other kind of relation to one another, such as colleague to colleague or superior to subordinate, are first and foremost individuals. To interactions with others they bring their own values and belief systems, and therefore their own assumptions as to larger purpose. *Leadership occurs when one member in the relation causes the other to see and affirm an understanding of how a given task or behavior serves the common good.* The leadership phenomenon does not require that entire value systems be changed, but it does require that some sharing of belief or value relative to the common good is either revealed or created. It may be that the sharing need not even be conscious. In any case, it is not merely temporary, because if genuine, it has to do with one's understanding of the world and not just with utility. It will persist after the relation until it is either forgotten or replaced by a competing understanding.

An ethical challenge is confronted when one or more members of a collective see a conflict between the goal or means and the *common* good, even if the goal and means both clearly serve the *collective* good. So it is that leadership must begin with a concerted effort to discover or create shared understandings of how goals and means serve the common good. With hard work, shared understandings can often be found, but leaders respect individual autonomy when these efforts fail. In such situations, they know that integrity requires that something give way. If acceptable alternatives are not to be found, the task, sometimes even the relationship itself, must be abandoned. The language used here is innocuous, but it describes both small and large expressions of integrity, including the supreme example of moral commitment: the case where one risks or sacrifices life itself for his or her convictions. In a world of purpose, survival is a concern, but it is not the ultimate concern.

Convictions don't complicate the equation when members are not concerned about the common good, but leadership is not involved in such situations, either. A different sort of relation then occurs. Influence is still at work, but *management* describes the interaction with those members. This complex phenomenon is considered next.

The Mystical Mixture: Management, Influence, Leadership

Leadership does not occur where there is no more or less shared conception of the common good. Much democratic management passes for leadership when in fact the "leader" brings to the relation no commitment to any particular conception of purpose or the common good other than what polls or the market say will be most profitable. In both politics and business, individuals often temporarily, superficially adopt particular values because doing so is likely to improve popularity (electability) or profit margins, but management, not leadership, is then the correct name for what is taking place.

But a vast amount of collaborative activity of yet another sort occurs that also does not conform to the foregoing definition of leadership. These interactions, too, are in most cases best understood as forms or products of management. If members in the relation see neither the collective's goals nor the means to those goals as serving the common good, only management takes place. This raises an important question often overlooked in current writing about leadership. What are the dynamics of the interface between management and leadership? Does management *turn into* leadership? If so, how does this happen?

Typical superior-subordinate relationships are management relationships. Collective goals can be shared for a variety of reasons. Collaborative action in pursuit of those goals occurs, and may even be highly effective, but the relationship is purely managerial if there is no shared conception of a larger good. If one member, however, understands his or her activity in the relation as furthering both the collective good *and* the common good (via either means or ends), a particular sort of *influence* is also at work. There is immediate potential for leadership to occur. Leadership invades the relation when the other member adopts or moves toward that same understanding. It can move the opposite direction as well, from leadership to management, if the influence becomes sufficient-ly negative. Either way, the qualitative nature of the relationship changes.

External influence of many kinds can also initiate the relationship, a point we will return to below. Influence thus understood is the link—the *causal factor*—between management and leadership. Exactly when and how the "transformation" then occurs, to use Burns's term, is impossible to describe empirically. Perhaps it is best to classify it, as does Hodgkinson, as a mystery.

> [T]he mystery of leadership...may well involve the overcoming of the [the world of fact] (i.e., reality constraints) by the [world of value] (i.e. value creativity) to the end of new dimensions of cooperative accomplishment, new frontiers, new worlds of possibility.[34]

Some would-be leaders can effect such a transformation and some cannot. Some members are amenable to it, some are not. Those not amenable may well remain in the relation, even as enthusiastic, effective collaborators for the collective good, but their understanding of what is going on within the collective is not the same. Whereas one member sees the collective's ethical guidelines in relation to the common good, the other member sees them only as game rules—rules which improve efficiency by reducing ambiguity and facilitating evaluation of performance, but can be left at the door on the way out if one so chooses. Thus it is possible (and common) for leadership and management to occur simultaneously within the same work group or organization.

This is a dynamic, mystical mixture, and it exists at every level of organizations and every level of society. Referring back to the three types of managers described in chapter three (the manager, the "supermanager," and the "superman"), the potential for transformation is there for them all. Wherever the transforming influence comes from, the superman or superwoman can become a leader when purpose and meaning turn his or her unique artistic gifts or immense power resources to serve the common good. In like manner, the supermanager can become a leader who uses his or her organizational and people skills ethically, a leader who *has* values and vision rather than a supermanager who *uses* values and vision. The lower level manager or line worker becomes a leader when he knows that the collective's goals serve or do not conflict with the common good, and also grasps the ethical significance of means—the way he goes about his routine tasks. As young Ruby Bridges showed, leadership is not a function of age or rank.

Transforming Influence

Hyrum Smith, creator of the Franklin Day Planner, tells the story of an executive named Herman Krannert who in 1925 was summoned to a posh lunch with the president of the large company he worked for. Surprised and excited to receive such an invitation, Krannert was completely overwhelmed when, during lunch, the president announced that later that day Krannert would be promoted to senior executive vice-president, and that he would also become the newest member of the corporate board of directors. Once over his shock, Krannert enthusiastically promised to dedicate himself to making the company great. The president, pleased to hear this, then asked Krannert to remember one caveat: as a member of the board, he would be expected to vote exactly as the president told him to. Krannert gave it some thought, got angry, stood up, and announced that he would not work for such a company. He quit on the spot. Four nights later there was a knock at his door, and when he opened it, six senior executives from his former company burst in. Having heard what he had done, they had quit too, and had come to announce that they were coming to work for Krannert. Doing what, he wanted to know? "Oh, we figure you'll find something, and when you do, we're going to work for you." That night, around Krannert's dining room, the seven of them drew up plans for what would become an empire: the Inland Container Corporation.[35]

Those men had not worked for Krannert before; he had not been leading or managing them. They had been his colleagues, but his actions were sufficiently influential to precipitate a leadership relationship.

Rost sees influence as the intentional use of various power resources to persuade, but as Krannert's case illustrates, persuasion can also be wholly unplanned and unintentional. Rost's discussion of influence is useful because he recognizes it as an important component *inside* the leadership relation. Beyond Rost, though, influence seems to get little attention from other leadership theorists. This may be a result of Burns's unfortunate dismissal of it over 20 years ago. "I dispense with the concept of influence as unnecessary," he wrote.[36] This is not a helpful view. If leadership is a particular sort of relationship, it only makes sense to ask what drew followers into that relationship in the first place, and it makes sense to ask what *keeps* them there. Asking these questions is anything but splitting hairs. The answer in both cases is influence, and if the role of influence is ignored, the boundaries of leadership remain unclear.

Consider two of the definitions quoted above. Kouzes and Posner believe that leadership involves "mobilizing others to want to struggle for shared aspirations." For Fairholm, it is "influencing people to accomplish organizational goals." These statements seem to assume that leadership has begun even before the would-be followers have committed themselves to being led; that leadership begins at the first moment of contact between the two parties. But this skips over a critical period of time in which the potential followers are evaluating both the activity being proposed and the would-be leader. If leadership by definition involves mutual purpose, to use Rost's term, what is happening while the would-be followers decide whether to accept a purpose for themselves? They may well participate—in many cases they have no choice, because it's part of their job—but things don't become mutual until they too own that purpose. They don't become "followers" until then. Can leadership occur without followers? Surely not.

Like the non-hierarchical relationships in Krannert's case, superior-subordinate relationships in a typical organizational setting are initially transformed by something other than leadership, and that something is influence. Not just any kind of influence, but *ethical* influence. Here we come again to the fundamental argument of this book. It is an ethical action or idea, usually on the part of one individual, that influences others to enter the leadership relationship, and it is the continuation of that influence, against and over all other competing influences, that causes them to remain in it. Ethics thus both precedes and sustains leadership.

Living a life of integrity—living ethically—earns one the opportunity to lead. Continuing to live ethically earns one the opportunity to continue to lead. Leadership is what leaders and followers do collaboratively with those opportunities. According to this argument, authentic leadership is *always* "transforming," to use Burns's term, for by definition it involves larger meaning and purpose. Influence, however, may or may not be transforming. *Transforming influence* is the effective, causal link between some other kind of relationship and leadership. Positive, potentially transforming influence is a *product* of living ethically, while leadership itself is a specific *form* of ethical living.

The Story of Bill

Positive influence in the case of Herman Krannert has a parallel in the negative example of William Jefferson Clinton. Given the way the story finally played itself out in the 2000 presidential election, it is difficult to imagine a more dramatic or instructive case study.

Commentators agreed: minus Monica Lewinsky, George W. Bush's chances of defeating Albert Gore, Jr. would have fallen to somewhere between slim and none. Jack Germond of the *Baltimore Sun* expressed the consensus in saying that Gore lost an election "he should have won in a walk." It should have been the easiest of handoffs, from Bill to Al, for nearly everything was in their favor. The economy was booming at record levels, and the world situation presented no immediate threat to national security. "Peace and prosperity—that is supposed to be a winning combination," said one long-time congressional Democrat. The key issues were ones that both polls and strategists agreed should favor a Democratic candidate: education, environment, and entitlement programs such as Medicare and Social Security. Republicans had the edge only on taxes.[37] Respected analysts felt that Clinton was leaving the nation significantly stronger than when he took office: its finances, crime rates, environment and economy all had improved.[38] Further, veterans in both camps felt Bush was a much weaker candidate as far as understanding and articulating the issues. What then explains the Democrats' loss? Bill must have become Al's Achilles' heel.

But voter exit polls give reason to question that hypothesis. Clinton left office with a 65 percent approval rating, as high or higher than any other departing president.[39] How is it, then, that Gore could carry neither Clinton's state nor his own, even against an unimpressive opponent who finally carried his own brother's state only by the slimmest of margins? The election's outcome left many scratching their heads in amazement. Gore Vidal, one of the best-known literary figures of our time and a cousin of Al Gore, was among them. "The mystifying thing," Vidal said, "is how under any circumstances they could have made a viable candidate out of George Bush...how the race got close is beyond me—other than that Cousin Albert obviously has problems projecting himself. After 30, 40 years in politics, I don't see how it's possible."[40] Vidal was totally baffled by what happened, and he was not alone. As one pundit summarized it, "Virtually every poll was wrong."

There is much to ponder here.

At the time he left office, not every poll was in Clinton's favor. When asked if he was "honest and trustworthy," 67 percent of respondents in an ABC News-Washington Post poll said no. A November 7th (2000) exit poll found that for 44 percent of voters, Clinton's behavior was very or somewhat important in their evaluation of the candidates.[41] Unfortunately for Gore, that translated into guilt by association. One immediate answer, then, seems to be trust. Former Clinton aide George Stephanopoulos framed this dimension pointedly: "It's awkward to advise a man whom you don't fully respect, and it's unnerving to represent a man whom you don't fully trust."[42] Trust would seem to be the simple answer. Clinton's breach of it must have been of sufficient magnitude to swamp Gore, too.

That would be a misleadingly incomplete conclusion. If it were that simple, neither Vidal nor the pollsters would have been so puzzled. Other research seemed to indicate that such things need not be politically fatal. Exit polls during Clinton's 1996 contest with Bob Dole *already* had found that 67 percent of voters believed a politician could suffer from "substantial flaws in character" and still govern effectively.[43] The same poll indicated that 70 percent of voters felt Dole could be characterized as moral, but only 41 percent would say the same of Clinton. Yet, Clinton won that election by a margin of twelve states. What was the bottom line in 1996, at least for swing voters, if not morality?

The answer, according to Burns and Sorenson, was leadership. When voters were asked to rank five traits (competence, empathy, integrity, leadership, and negativity) as to their desirability in a presidential candidate, leadership ranked first.[44]

"Leadership" was left undefined in the poll question, but many of those polled wanted to know what was meant by the term. These questioners seemed to fall into two groups: those who felt leadership could be divorced from ethics or morals, and those who didn't. Those in the second category seemed to define leadership more along the lines of "brokering or managing," something that required no moral underpinnings. To use Burns's terminology again, such leadership would fall into the "transactional" category.

What is interesting in Burns and Sorenson's account is that the voters seemed to naturally understand this distinction. They already thought in terms of two categories: moral "leadership" and non-moral (but not necessarily *im*moral) "management or brokering." Given this awareness, and given Monica in the middle, one possible explanation for the differing outcomes in the two elections presents itself. American voters seem to understand not only that the presidency involves both kinds of responsibility, but also that the management side does not require moral rectitude to be done effectively. The 1996 election epitomized American pragmatism. The Whitewater scandal and Clinton's alleged earlier affairs had happened in Arkansas, but he seemed to be doing a little better since then—at least well enough to meet some minimum moral threshold on the leadership side. The management side, in any case, was strong and getting stronger.

Election 2000 was also an expression of American pragmatism, but this time the quantities in the equation were clearer. The extraordinary approval ratings in exit polls reflected appreciation of Clinton's impeccable political skill; he was truly great at the transactional stuff. He was leaving the country, at least materially, in pretty good shape. But in the election itself, voters addressed the leadership issue. Clinton no longer met the moral minimum. Had he been straight with them, rather than jabbing his finger at them, that probably would not have been the case. As one post-election analyst told Jim Lehrer on PBS, "People wanted Clinton to admit and ask forgiveness for his behavior, to have a sense of shame, to repent. But he never did. If he had, the

American people are enormously forgiving, and it would not have been an issue."[45] Presidents have to have at least a *hint* of moral awareness; have to represent *something* people and their children can look up to. Gore was guilty by association at the very least; guilty enough to offset a multitude of Bush weaknesses. The next president would have to be more than a manager.

Burns and Sorenson wrote in 1999 that "Clinton's knee-jerk political instinct was *survival* first, principles second."[46] As if to remove any remaining doubt, one of his last acts in office was an act of survival.[47] On his very last day in the White House, he brokered a deal with independent counsel Robert Ray to avoid indictment and criminal prosecution in the Lewinsky case, signing a statement admitting that "certain of my responses to questions about Ms. Lewinsky were false."[48] Clinton was a manager—or a "superman" creating his art—to the very end. The day before, in a televised farewell address to the nation, he had buoyantly proclaimed that he would leave the presidency "more idealistic, more full of hope" than the day he arrived.[49] His statement takes on additional meaning in light of the problem he resolved the next day.

How much need be said here? To state the obvious, private behavior, when it becomes public, is a form of influence. It has the power to transform constituents into followers, and followers back into constituents. Whether stemming from public or private behavior, influence determines the nature of the relationship. After the Lewinsky scandal, many Americans viewed Bill Clinton purely as America's manager, not as its leader. Fred Harburg of General Motors has expressed concern about the extent to which the media use "the character dimension of leadership" to stalk public figures like predators waiting for the kill.[50] There is truth in that statement. On the other hand, people understandably want to know what type of person they are dealing with. They want to know the terms of the relationship.

The Leader's Undivided World: *Public* and *Private*

Bernard Bass describes trust as "the single most important variable" related to the effectiveness of transformational leadership. The trust "so necessary" for such leadership is lost "when the leader is caught in a lie."[51] Research conducted by Kouzes and Posner over the past two decades strongly supports this argument. Literally thousands of business and government executives, primarily from North America but also from Asia, Europe and Australia, were asked what values (personal traits or characteristics) they looked for and most admired in superiors. The answers, say Kouzes and Posner, have shown "striking regularity" over the years. From among 225 different values, traits, and characteristics, honesty tops the list. In 1995, 88 percent of respondents listed it, more than ten percentage points higher than any other response. In 1987, the gap was over 20 percent. Honesty is the cornerstone of integrity and credibility, which are in turn basic elements of leadership.

But isn't honesty on the job enough? What is the relationship between a leader's private behavior and his or her public effectiveness? Like the Hitler question, this one has always generated lively discussion, and the Clinton experience has only fueled the debate. In a world of purpose, there is just one answer. If leadership can correctly be understood as ethical living writ large, the private/public dichotomy resolves itself: there can be no contradiction between them. One of the assumptions of the theory of leadership being presented here is that before leaders can be leaders, they must be ethical individuals in some sense. What is private precedes and shapes what is public.

This does not mean that leaders are expected never to fail, either privately or publicly, but the way they deal with failure when it does come is a critical element of influence with respect to the nature of the leader-follower relation. Nor does it mean that good character automatically translates into effective leadership. Leaders must have a number of skills in order to be effective; Kouzes and Posner and others address the skill dimension well. It does not mean that leaders' private lives should be known to others, but for the reasons outlined below, what might be found there must resonate with what is already public. Finally, it does not mean that leaders don't manage. All leaders *must* manage to a greater or lesser extent. If their management skills are poor, they still must manage well enough to select collaborators who will make up for those weaknesses. How leaders manage will reflect their personal ethical commitments.

Much has been written about the importance of consistency of character to a leader's effectiveness in the workplace, so we need not focus on that aspect of the public/private question here. One of the best texts on that topic is *Leadership and the Quest for Integrity*. Authors Joseph Badaracco and Richard Ellsworth capture the bottom line nature of ethics for leaders on the job.

> [E]thical standards form the core of the ideal organization [because] these ethical standards are personal. They reflect the attitudes, judgments, experiences, and values of men and women responsible for leading companies. Ethical standards are the crucial link between leaders' aims for their organizations, on the one hand, and their own personal beliefs and actions, on the other. And integrity...is fundamentally a matter of coherence and consistency among organizational aims, personal values and beliefs, and individual behavior. ... [T]he companies to which outstanding leaders commit their effort, intelligence, and attention are expressions of themselves. Because they closely identify with their organizations, these leaders seek to make their companies expressions of the beliefs and values they hold important.[52]

These are crucial points, and many good books echo them. But these books generally fail to step back further to couch their arguments in the larger context of ethics *per se*. More specifically, there are three unavoidable ethical implications that follow from what Badaracco and Ellsworth are saying, but they are rarely spelled out in black and white.

First, there is the implication of *means*, or the *methods and tools* of management. In the statement above, these are addressed in terms of the link between "aims" and "actions." Leaders, often with the help of followers, specify ends, but they also specify the means to those ends. Some means are simply not acceptable; they violate the personal values and beliefs that make up the leader's personal ethical system. So it is that both means and ends are expressions of the purpose necessarily embodied in that ethical system. Unless this point is fully appreciated, the frequent and powerful temptation to violate means constraints in order to achieve desired ends will win out. Extensively using "temporary" employees to save money by avoiding more appropriate, long-term commitments to them is an example. *Means are just as important as ends, for they express and inculcate an organization's identity, and shape the personal identities of its members. Means can themselves be a form of progress and achievement.* Means constraints must apply not only within the organization, but outside it as well, in the private realm. Ethical principles are more than game rules: they are grounded in a larger understanding of the purpose and meaning of life. A value is not a value if one leaves work without it.

Second is the implication of *ends*. "Coherence" among aims, personal values, beliefs and behavior implies there is no conflict between the organization's goals or activities and the leader's private understanding of the common good. Where possible, those goals directly pursue that conception of the common good (which likely has been further refined as a result of interaction with followers). Of course, if a superior's belief system rests upon the eat-or-be-eaten maxim of the survival paradigm, that so-called "common good" is simply either the invisible hand of the market or the visible hand of brute force. In this view, if the organization should not survive, the market will ultimately say so. Until then, its claim to a right to exist is beyond question. Serving the collective (organizational) good, in other words, is as close as this view comes to the common good. Advertising agencies willing to deceive consumers or violate their rights in other ways are one example. The dumping of harmful products in unprotected markets is another. True leaders and followers, on the other hand, because they recognize a larger common good, are obligated by a higher standard. They must constantly evaluate both the organization's processes and products.

The third implication relates to our quick survey in chapter two of the modern dichotomy between *public* and *private* worlds. Urbanization, mechanization, specialization, mass marketing/production/consumption and economic science have all contributed to individual alienation. Production can be a purely public act, devoid of either purpose or a personal dimension, a problem made even worse when shareholder return takes precedence over authentic customer service. The law of the market as a morally neutral, objective "fact" easily divorces the public world of "facts" from the private world of faith, value, or purpose. The ethical grounding of leadership provides a basis for combating this alienation via a focused effort to re-unite the public and the private worlds.

In answer to the question, "Does the private behavior of a leader matter?" the leader answers, "Uniting those two realms is an essential function of leadership." Defining the purpose of the organization in terms of service to the common good gives meaning to the work being done. What is being done, and the way in which it is being done, is for a reason. This is something people can take home with them. What they bring from home, too, can be validated as useful in the workplace if they find in the would-be leader's vision of the common good some overlap with their own, pre-existing vision. They can then enthusiastically contribute to the realization of that vision.

However logical this may seem, the assumption of a public/private divorce is deeply engrained in modern society. Suggesting that one's private life should have anything at all to do with one's identity at work is now offensive to some. Yet, like the idea of leadership outlined above, the argument that leadership also involves concordance between public and private is not new. More than 2,400 years ago, Socrates told his listeners that "The first key to greatness is to be in reality what we appear to be." Just a few years earlier, on the opposite side of the globe, Confucius had taught his followers that the good of the state and the welfare of society depended upon leaders conducting themselves properly in all activities, public and private. The three implications of leadership as ethics discussed above relate to integrity, a term which literally means "completeness" or "unity." The potential to positively influence others by adhering to principle in public is greatly reduced if that adherence is not also consistently practiced in private. The ethical self is an integrated, undivided self, and so is the ethical leader.

There is one other dimension to be mentioned here: the dimension of performance. Badaracco and Ellsworth note that, in an organizational context, widely and genuinely held values can markedly improve communication, decision-making, and the evaluation of personnel and projects. When people know that trust, fairness, and respect characterize the environment, they are more likely to feel secure enough to attempt new and better things.

> When serving a worthwhile, creative purpose, employees can become intensely committed to satisfying customers' needs. Ultimately this is the bedrock of competitive advantage.[53]

This is encouraging but dangerous knowledge. If the desire to improve performance leads to the instrumental use of values as mere tools, it will show. For example, if "open door" policies are in fact a means of identifying potential troublemakers, or "respect for the individual" is only a mantra to *attract* faithful employees rather than as axiom for corporate behavior *toward* employees, those employees will figure it out. If an organization's commitment to ethical principles is less than genuine, those principles will ultimately become a source of and target for sarcasm. Given time, people can distinguish leadership from management. Properly ordered, a potential leader's ethical commitments guide his or her organizational commitments, not the other way around. Values must be adopted because they are right, not because they are productive.

In concluding this look at the connection between public and private, it is important to point out that nearly everything said here applies to followers as much as, if not more than, it does to leaders. As business consultant Robert Kelley has noted, this is true because the ethical dimension of leadership carries significant personal implications for followers. If they had no part in choosing the course of action, subordinates are in essence being told to do what someone else *has already decided* ought to be done. When leaders or managers make decisions independently, as they sometimes must, they "deem the level of morality acceptable" not only for themselves but also for those who are to carry out those decisions.[54] Subordinates, therefore, need a special brand of moral courage.

Kelley tells us that followers account for 80 to 90 percent of organizational effectiveness. If this is so, it is surely also true that they account for the same proportion of an organization's integrity. When given instructions they cannot morally condone, all employees, and especially those nearest the top of an organization, have tremendous moral responsibility. Herman Krannert's case above illustrates just such a situation, and also illustrates the latent potential for leadership in every superior-subordinate interaction. His ethical response to unethical instructions was the genesis of leadership. Subordinates who act ethically by refusing to do what is unethical, or, as is often more productive and responsible, suggest or take alternative positive action, act individually with integrity and, in so doing, protect the integrity of the organization. *To the extent that their influence causes others to act in a similar manner, they also lead.*

Subordinates who allow their superiors to do their ethical decision-making for them are morally lazy. Superiors who do not make it easier for subordinates to express concerns and suggest alternatives are irresponsible and insensitive. Leaders and followers may have agreed on a given ethical end, but leaders must not assume that any given means to that end is also therefore acceptable to all followers. The moral strength of an organization turns on the extent to which subordinates and followers—not just managers and leaders—remain faithful in public to what they believe in private.

Practical Applications

To this point our discussion has been largely hypothetical. At least for a few pages, we should "get down to brass tacks." It has been argued that leadership by definition serves the common good, either in terms of means, ends, or both. What are some practical applications of leadership as ethics? More specifically, in light of contemporary realities and movements, what are the foremost challenges facing individuals who adopt such an understanding of leadership? Although conceptions of the common good will differ to some degree, some specific answers to these questions can be suggested. They lie in both the public and private realms, and they are extremely important.

Perhaps the most obvious public direction for contemporary leadership is economic. Leadership theorist Robert Wren tells of James Madison's struggle with the question of how best to serve the common good in light of the threat of factions. Specifically, Madison wrestled with how to secure both the public good (loosely equated with majority rule) while at the same time protecting the private rights of individuals and those not among the majority. We must find, said Madison, "a republican remedy for the diseases most incident to a republican government."[55] His solution was a good one: the American constitutional system. Today, larger players in the global economy sometimes have overly negative effects on the supply of resources or on groups and nations not strong enough to dictate the terms of their own participation in the global economy. The global market is a product of the survival paradigm, and where there are no restraints (such as are in place domestically), the strong often consume the livelihood of the less fit. We can revise Madison's question and ask, "Is there a capitalist solution for the diseases most incident to a capitalist system?"

Given that pretext, a convenient entry point into practical economic leadership is found in a 1992 *Business Quarterly* article by Manuel Velasquez, recently reprinted in DesJardins and McCall's popular classroom text, *Contemporary Issues in Business Ethics*. Velasquez concludes his article, "International Business, Morality, and the Common Good," with these words.

> What endures is each organization's single-minded pursuit of increasing its profits in a competitive environment. ...[I]t is not obvious that we can say that multinationals have an obligation to contribute to the global common good in a competitive environment in the absence of an international authority that can force all agents to contribute to the global common good.[56]

He reaches this conclusion on the basis of a particular "ethical" premise: "when others do not adhere to the requirements of morality it is not immoral for one to do likewise."[57] In the vernacular, if other companies are doing it, yours can too. Leadership, as we have defined it here, must unequivocally reject such a view. This is because, despite using the form of ethical argument, Velasquez holds to another, more telling underlying premise that belies his position's non-ethical substance. That is, he equates corporate identity with individual identity, and the corporate right to survive with the individual (human) right to survive. Thus, he assumes that corporate survival is justified under all market circumstances, and further assumes that rational action, either corporate or individual, can therefore be defined as self-protective action. These assumptions ensconce his view securely in the survival paradigm, and in that paradigm, ethics are optional. In that context, articles about "ethics" are a waste of time unless they have market value. He is writing about game rules. Genuine ethical premises are of a qualitatively different nature.

Leaders act just as game rules predict they should *not* act. From the perspective of the survival paradigm, they act irrationally.

We need only return again to Gandhi and King to illustrate this point. By every conceivable application of Velasquez's premises, the behaviors of these men and their followers were irrational. Given the danger of what they undertook and the greatness of the odds against them, these two leaders did not act so as to protect themselves or to acquire material things, and neither did their followers. Their inspiring stories need not be retold here, but the relevant point bears repeating. Leaders don't act "rationally" per the norms of the survival paradigm, for survival is not their ultimate value. Survival alone is not enough.

Business leaders, if they are truly leaders, also make "irrational" decisions. A company's immorality cannot be justified simply by pointing to the immoral actions of other companies. Velasquez concludes that until an international authority strong enough to "force" corporations to respect the common good comes along, they can—and rationally *should*—continue to ignore that good when it hurts competitive advantage. There are two immediate reactions here. First, he apparently assumes that such an international authority will come along before irreversible, if not fatal, damage is done to the environment or to weaker nations. Depletion of natural resources would be an example. Second, he seems to assume that such authorities—those with the power to effectively *force* certain types of corporate behavior—already exist somewhere.

Both conclusions are disingenuous. There are few signs that the first assumption will bear out, but does that then mean there is no more we can do? Surely not. As to the second, there are only two *truly* effective constraints on corporate behavior: one is the market itself, the other is corporations themselves. We cannot afford to wait and hope for some ill-defined, and in all likelihood ineffective, international authority to materialize and make everyone act responsibly. Ethicist Richard DeGeorge has outlined ten ethical strategies for dealing with corruption; firms with integrity have the moral courage to use them.[58] In sum, corporate boards, CEO's and shareholders face a difficult decision: whether to operate in the survival paradigm, or to operate in a world of purpose. More concisely, they must choose between managing and leading.

There is sometimes more than a little truth in the joke about "business ethics" being an oxymoron. Velasquez's argument and his conclusions are notable examples. If one reasons within the survival paradigm, ethical constraints have no ground. Whatever constraints do exist will either be game rules, terms of contracts, or products of tradition, and will be selected according to utility. There are, however, approaches to business ethics which do assume a world of purpose, but the determinative premises are not always easy to spot.[59] Even in texts that assume purpose, the point being made here is often overlooked because the focus is typically on case studies involving difficult choices between "right and right." Some of these works are excellent for their intended purpose. Badaracco's *Defining Moments: When Managers Must Choose Between Right and Right* is one.[60] But the biggest issues confronting leaders and followers today are not of that sort. The biggest issues are simpler, in that what is right is undeniably clear, but they are also more difficult, for doing what is right may significantly affect the bottom line. The entertainment industry provides a representative example.

In 1999, a six-year old girl died of injuries that, according to one description, were worse than those seen in many automobile collisions. The child suffered severe liver damage, a broken rib, and a badly fractured skull in addition to multiple cuts and bruises. She had been kicked and slugged repeatedly. Prosecutors charged her assailant with first-degree murder. The 12-year old boy who killed the girl said he did so accidentally while imitating professional wrestlers.[61]

Among young males between the ages of 12 and 24, the World Wrestling Federation's "Monday Night Raw" cable telecasts during the Fall 2000 season beat ABC's "Monday Night Football" by 47 percent.[62] We have been down similar roads before, and as before, science is preparing signposts for the crossroads we are approaching on this one. One such previous road dealt with tobacco advertising aimed at minors. Laboratory science provided solid evidence linking tobacco use to cancer, and social science established the effectiveness of ad campaigns on children and youth. Ultimately, non-corporate leaders had to step forward to begin the process of preventing advertising which influenced persons under the age of 18, and of punishing the tobacco industry for its harmful and immoral tactics. Similarly, research is now beginning to show direct links between television violence viewed during early childhood and more aggressive behavior exhibited subsequently throughout a child's life. A recent report by the U.S. Surgeon General concludes that violent television programming and video games are harmful to children.[63] Given solid empirical data, if leaders again do not step forward from within the industry in question, leaders from other quarters will be urgently needed to do for them the work of developing and implementing appropriate controls. Leadership relative to the entertainment industry is now a front burner issue.

There are three other critical points in the economic sphere to touch upon. One, already mentioned above in the comments of Peter Drucker, is the need for businesses to accept responsibility for their role in the world as employer, neighbor and citizen. This is especially true in light of the violence issue. To repeat his basic point, "It is futile to argue, as does...Nobel laureate Milton Friedman...that a business has only one responsibility: economic performance." That is, business *must* have more than one purpose; the survival paradigm is inadequate. Drucker is right for the reasons outlined in the response to Velasquez above, and simply because, in the modern world, "organizations collectively *are* society."[64] This is another challenge for today's leaders.

Any progress on the first point may depend heavily upon the second, which is the development of a similar perspective among shareholders. *Share*holders are only one group of *stake*holders in corporate activity, but they hold enormous power. Johnson and Johnson's corporate "credo" is often held up as a model that appropriately conditions that power because it provided the foundation for an ethical response to the Tylenol crisis some years ago. A key element in that credo is responsibility to the world community. Shareholders are the last group in the credo's listing of stakeholders. Ethical business involves not violating that priority order of value. Hewlett-Packard's "Statement of Corporate Objectives" also explicitly states an obligation to world society. Whether or not these corporate giants generally achieve such lofty goals, their corporate statements of responsibility provide a framework for pursuing them. The challenge for business leaders is to convince both employees and shareholders to adopt such statements and take them seriously.

Finally, there is a pressing need for leaders with the wisdom and insight to carefully re-evaluate modern assumptions regarding economic growth. Increased production is usually accepted as an end in itself, as marketing and strategic planning seek to foster the rapid obsolescence (or perceived obsolescence) that will motivate further production and consumption. We must think seriously about how long we should (or can) continue in this direction.

> Growth is for the sake of growth and is not determined by any overarching social purpose. And that, of course, is an exact account of the phenomenon which, when it occurs in the human body, is called cancer. ... [T]he exuberant capitalism of the past 250 years will be diagnosed in the future as a desperately dangerous case of cancer in the body of human society....[65]

These are sobering words, and the challenge is complex. We have seen in the past century that planned economies stifle initiative and adaptation. Leaders with extraordinary creativity are needed to discern new models for growth that are less pathological but still recognize the importance of incentive and competition.

The extreme mobility of employees in the modern economy is a hugely complicating factor for all three of these issues. The dean of business at one major university compares today's careers in business to free agency in professional sports.

> The best way to equip students for [globalization] is to give them the tools to function at peak efficiency at a very early stage.... They're highly mobile and don't expect to remain with one team. Training periods are minimal. They have to perform impressively from the start. And they are more likely than ever to move to a new job after a year or two.[66]

Velasquez argues that employee mobility is one reason why corporations are unable to consistently focus on any objective other than profit. If he is correct, then that mobility contributes to corporate irresponsibility, and business programs in colleges and universities need to be doing something greater than just giving students the tools to move around effectively.

This brings us to another practical application of these ideas to business leadership. DeGeorge observes that "companies that act with integrity are largely a function of individuals within...who act with integrity."[67] Educational institutions must recognize and assume their responsibility for preparing students to be such individuals. Schools do little more than help to prove Velasquez right if they only equip students with skills, and fail to confront them with the paradigmatic differences between leadership and management. That might be a requisite first step. In light of Drucker's points, a second step might be to actually *discourage* mobility because of its deleterious effects not only on companies, but also on communities, families, and on employees themselves. Lack of a sense of place makes personal alienation that much harder to overcome. Identity and commitment suffer apart from a sense of rootedness and ownership. Corporations, too, like educational institutions, need to have the vision and moral courage to link the mobility factor to any stated commitment to society. Allowing and encouraging employees to stay in one place for longer periods of time is one way to directly serve the common good.

Looking in another direction, we face pressing questions related to new doors science has now placed before us. As the pace of change accelerates beyond our control, the answers demand great care and resolve. More than thirty years ago, ethicist Paul Ramsey framed one of these questions as science began taking steps toward the awesome capability of generating human life in a laboratory, and the consequent opportunity to either terminate it or preserve it alive as the subject of an experiment. Scientists themselves have drawn attention to the "ethical questions" looming here. But a scientist's conscience is entirely "frivolous," Ramsey suggests,

> ...if he is not at the same time, and in advance, prepared to stop the whole procedure should the "ethical finding" concerning this fact-situation turn out to be, for any serious conscience, murder. It would perhaps be better not to raise the ethical issues, than not to raise them in earnest.[68]

This is surely one of the most important areas of responsibility for leaders of our time. Our scientific and technological prowess has brought us face to face with ourselves. We must raise the ethical issues in earnest. Leaders guide us as we forge ahead, but in ethical directions *only*. They help us alter our course—or stop—when "the ethical finding" is that we have made a wrong turn or gone too far. Leaders determine when to say no. This is not an elitist view of leadership, because average citizens may have the most responsibility of all in confronting such questions.

Before concluding this section, a bit more can be said with respect to individual responsibility both public and private. If leadership is a category of ethics, then leaders are first and foremost ethical individuals. Ethical individuals who act in a group setting have the potential to lead—to serve the common good—in the way they fulfill even the most routine organizational duties, no matter where they work. At the same time, they recognize that this is not enough. Ethics demands that they also honestly evaluate the relationship of collective goals to the common good. When there is a conflict, ethical individuals act with integrity to resolve that conflict, but, if resolution seems impossible, they may have no other choice than to leave the organization. Staying on the payroll of a company that produces, distributes or markets a harmful product, for example, would be an implicit declaration of their own moral approval of that activity. Corporate consultant James Autry captures this idea powerfully.

> I take very seriously the role of business and its impact on society. I shudder when I hear some businessperson say, "It's just business," because that usually means something is being done in the name of business that would not be done if that person were doing it in the name of himself or herself. Always remember this: If we can commit an injustice in the name of business, we can commit an injustice in the name of anything.[69]

Despite fervent claims to the contrary, we do not leave parts of our individual selves behind at the end of the work day. We are what we do.

Autry also ventures into the uncharted waters of private life in a published letter to his son, Art. Noting that "society generally supports work life to a much greater degree than it supports family life," he advises Art to look for a company or career that does support families. Or, at the very least, to "avoid a company that rewards you for neglecting your family life."[70] Autry tells his son that families must not be sacrificed for careers, but observes, too, that not everything can be blamed on employers. Many employees, he says, invest more effort in making their work lives fulfilling than they invest in making their home and family lives fulfilling. This observation has the ring of truth to it. When confronted with a problem or challenge at work, most of us immediately shift into high gear, reading trade journals, holding formal and informal strategy sessions, calling in consultants and so on in an effort to resolve the problem or meet the challenge. For whatever reason, our response is qualitatively different at home. We seem less committed to those we should care about most.

What does the private dimension have to do with leadership? Two things, the first of which is integrity. If we care about and are kind to people at work, we need to do the same at home. If we keep promises at work, we need to do the same outside the workplace. If we listen intently at work, we need to do the same in our homes and communities. The second point speaks to superiors who have the power to impact the private dimension by uprooting employees and their families—or by separating them for long periods of time—in the name of efficiency. Work demands which unreasonably impact employees' families or support systems represent a conflict between the common good (represented by the welfare of an employee's private circle) and the collective good (represented by the corporate bottom line). Sociologists are placing another signpost in our path, one that will show that the disintegration of families and private support systems has negative consequences on society as a whole.[71] So it is that actions for or against the health of private relationships directly impact the common good. Progress sometimes disguises itself as stability.

Part IV

CONCLUSION

The only core of all our actions—if they are to be moral—is responsibility. Responsibility to something higher than my family, my country, my firm, my success.
— Vaclav Havel

6

How Do Leaders Survive?

I am not always bound to win but I am bound to be true. I am not always bound to succeed but I am bound to live up to what light I have. – Abraham Lincoln

Here I stand, I cannot do otherwise. – Martin Luther

Every one to whom much is given, of that person will much be required. – The Gospel of Luke

How Do Leaders Survive?

How is it that some leaders are able to remain true to their purposes in the face of powerful persons, systems or forces that don't recognize those purposes? Part of the answer has to do with finding genuine purpose in the first place. It is impossible to lead in any part of our lives without having done so.

With respect to leadership at work, however, this statement may pose a problem for people whose jobs, at least on the surface, appear to involve providing a luxury of some kind rather than meeting obvious biological or material needs. Can people whose vocations have to do with "luxuries" be leaders? They can, but in important ways that leadership has to do more with means than ends. Surviving as a leader in such a vocation requires that one consistently do things right, and that is more difficult than it sounds.

The week beginning Thursday, June 29 in the year 2000 was one basketball fans at the University of Kansas will not soon forget. The head coaching job at the University of North Carolina had just been offered to Kansas coach Roy Williams, and for a multitude of reasons, nearly everyone—even his own son—was sure Williams would take it. Leaving Kansas would likely have meant more fame, more money, the fulfillment of a life-long dream, and, after more than a decade away, once again residing close to family and old friends. He turned the job down. The decision drew so much national attention that National Public Radio's Susan Stamberg chose Williams as one of four persons to interview for a *Morning Edition* series focusing on leadership. Asked why he said no to North Carolina, Williams explained it this way:

> I had gone through my life dreaming of playing there and dreaming of coaching at North Carolina, and the most important reason for staying was because of my relationship with my players, both the current players and—maybe even more importantly—the *former* players that I had sold the idea of coming to Kansas. "Let's build what they already have at North Carolina. Let's build this family." It was the worst seven days of my life…because I knew I was going to upset or disappoint some people at both places. But the idea of not sticking with what I'd been preaching and teaching for twelve years, I couldn't handle.[1]

It seems fair to say that if his purpose in coaching boiled down to carrying out a job description, Williams's decision would have been simple. North Carolina was his childhood home and first love, so what better place could there be to do that job? At some point, however, he came face to face with the difference between doing a job and doing something more than a job. Things he had said to current players were important, but he also had to consider what he had told those long gone from Lawrence. On the basis of something larger than winning basketball games, he had *influenced* both current and former players to enter into a leader-follower relationship with him. His choice seems to have come down to what it would take for him to legitimately continue to view himself as that leader.

Williams's decision had a powerful effect on players who had recently joined the team. "We just went over the top in respect for him," said sophomore-to-be Drew Gooden. The decision also influenced future players. "What he showed me was he has character," said top high school prospect Aaron Miles, who later signed a letter of intent to play at Kansas. More surprisingly, perhaps only coincidentally, similar decisions made by other coaches were soon reported. Four weeks later, Cincinnati coach Bob Huggins turned down a professional coaching opportunity, saying, "I have made commitments to players, families and the community that I would like to see through." Less than two weeks after Williams made his choice, Minnesota coach Dan Monson said, "I'm a Catholic...it's a great, great opportunity...," then turned down an offer from Notre Dame—center of the sports universe for Catholic fans—because at the end of the previous season he had promised his players he would stay. Sam Donnellon of the *Philadelphia Daily News* then castigated another high-profile coach for not turning down a plum job the way Monson did. In an obvious reference to Williams, the coach in question had earlier defended his actions by saying loyalty could be to different things, but he wanted to be loyal to his family. But it can be argued that coaches also have to think about loyalty to families other than their own, and Donnellon's response is worth quoting.

> Fine. Then when someone offers you a five-year contract, say you only want to sign for one year. When a mother looks you in the eye and asks, "Will you be my son's coach all four years?" tell her about how your wife is from [the place you really want to be], how you think of it as a second home, how if they ever come calling, you'd leave quicker than one of

[Michael Jordan]'s cartoon co-stars. Tell them all the things you told those giddy people in [the place where you just took your new job].[2]

Maybe these are all coincidence, but then again, maybe not. Leaders have an impact. They lead their followers, and influence others as well. It is a responsibility not to be taken lightly.

The point is subtle, but it is absolutely critical to the philosophy of leadership being expounded in this book. When a superior recruits subordinates to join him or her in a project whose ostensible goal (in this case, the winning of basketball games) does not directly address obvious societal needs, the common good can still be significantly served if one condition is met: the pursuit of the goal must be conducted according to ethical principles. If the goal is pursued ethically, the stage is set for leadership to occur. It happens at the point where subordinates catch the vision of how life ought to be lived—how things, *any* things, ought to be done—and choose to join in the pursuit of that vision. Consistently acting according to principle is an expression of purpose and meaning. It is leadership by means, it can be done by almost anyone, and it has an impact. Leaders survive as leaders by saying yes to what is right in every circumstance, even when it means saying no to other highly desirable things.

More commonly, however, we think of leaders in terms of end goals that directly relate to larger societal issues. Looking back at some high profile, exemplary leaders of the past, certain things seem to stand out as having been keys to their ability to survive against all odds. It is enlightening, for example, to compare and contrast the lives of Lincoln and Gandhi. Gandhi was trying to start a revolution, Lincoln essentially trying to thwart one. Gandhi wanted certain people out of his country, Lincoln wanted to keep a large sector from seceding. Both men were dealing with, as Gandhi called it, "the deep disease of color prejudice," and both were committed to rooting it out, even at great cost.[3] Both were successful leaders, but both lost their lives because of their commitment to the common good.

Other similarities could be noted as well, but there is also an important difference that bears on our discussion. Gandhi had two ideological battles to fight, one right after the other. The first was against the British. Getting his fellow citizens to adhere to prin-ciples of nonviolence was difficult, but motivating them to rise up against their foreign masters was much less so. Although Gandhi in his own mind was serving a universal principle, a common good principle, most of his followers were not. Average Indians hated the "Britishers." For them, it was collective versus collective, a struggle against an enemy rather than for the common good. That was a problem, and Gandhi knew it. From hating the British, it was only a short step to hating their fellow countrymen. Gandhi fought mightily after independence to keep India united, but the challenge of uniting Hindus and Muslims was far more difficult than Lincoln's challenge of keeping North and South together. After winning the first ideological battle, Gandhi lost the second. In the wake of much bloodshed, some of which still continues today, India was divided.

Gandhi and Lincoln illustrate commitment to the common good, but Gandhi's story and the history of India also highlight the importance of carefully monitoring collective action to make sure sight of the common good is not lost. And he illustrates what was said earlier about success. Though he did not achieve one of his two primary goals, Gandhi was not a failure. Though a Hindu himself, he never gave in to the demands of Hindu nationalism; he did not simply do what the Hindu majority wanted. He was as successful as any one person could have been. Neither he nor Lincoln survived physically, but both are still seen as leaders today because they remained true to their common good purposes.

The leadership opportunities most of us face will likely not be as large as those of Lincoln and Gandhi, but we do not know what will confront us from one day to the next. Personal integrity and leadership in small things always precedes leadership in larger ones. Mother Teresa's story is familiar to us all, which in itself is something to think about. How is it that a quiet individual, committed simply to caring for lepers and outcasts, the most destitute of the destitute, could become such an international household name? She was true to her purpose, and now the entire world knows her.

There is another important lesson to be drawn from her example. Leaders survive as leaders by being willing to face conflict. It is not commonly known that Mother Teresa faced threats of physical violence during her early years of work in India. She and her coworkers were often seen as representatives of a foreign religion encroaching on Hindu territory.[4] Her continuing work in the face of hostile opposition is only part of the lesson. According to the ancient Hindu law of karma, there is no such thing as injustice in the human condition. Those who suffer or prosper now do so because they are reaping the fruit of their actions in previous lives. Was Mother Teresa, as an outsider, showing respect for traditional Hindu ideas by helping untouchables who "deserved" their lot in life? Some Hindus did not think so. Leaders have to make difficult choices in order to survive as such.

All leaders who survive have a source of strength and resolve so strong and real that it keeps them true to their purpose in difficult circumstances. For such persons, success is not defined in terms of achieving goals. Rather, it is measured by the correctness of their goals and by the means used to pursue them. Whether a matter of means or of both ends and means, a leader's effectiveness depends on an unwavering inner commitment to what is right.

Reflections

Early in his acclaimed book *On Leadership*, John Gardner steps back to survey the topic and makes an important observation. He sees leadership as a subtopic of a larger topic that he identifies as "the accomplishment of group purpose."[5] Groups accomplish their purposes in many different ways; leadership is just one of those ways. Similarly, this book categorizes leadership as a subtopic within a larger category, but the category is a different one: it is ethics. It has been argued here that leadership is best located within ethics; that leadership is one way of living an ethical life. If this is true, then the basic leadership concept itself—not just subcategories of leadership given special names—should be defined in ethical terms.

The formulations of leadership offered by Burns, Rost and Greenleaf have endured because each is somehow rooted in the true, ethical soil of leadership. We recognize something right in those definitions. Leadership is a mystical thing, extremely difficult to pin down, but we sense that in some necessary way it has to do with guiding others toward what is good. We *know* that true leaders do this, for it is the only way to define authentic progress. And we know that those who do not do this are not really leaders. Presenting the main idea of the first chapter in reverse emphasizes the point in a different way: if leadership does not necessarily include ethics, or if the "ethical principles" leaders promote only apply within the context of a particular group, what *significant* difference is there between leadership and management?

A great deal of time was spent in chapter two attempting to flesh out the more extreme aspects of the survival paradigm. This was done to highlight the profound qualitative difference between leadership and management. Perhaps because we are seldom physically confronted with it, or because we have become jaded after seeing repetitive violence in the media, many of us in the modern world lack a real appreciation of the brutality of the survival paradigm. We are relatively comfortable with science because science is curing our diseases and making our lives more comfortable. But science is only a tool, and though it is often put to good uses, this is not due to something in its own nature. Science can also describe or facilitate horrible things without a trace of emotion.

Leadership comes from a different world. Management is to leadership as problem-solving is to purpose-serving; as information is to meaning; as survival is to service. How is it that we have come to the point of so easily using the two words interchangeably? We fail to grasp how different their origins are. Until we learn to wed leadership and ethics in our minds, the difference between leadership and management is only quantitative, a function of varying skill sets. Until then, leadership can be reduced to a technology. Until then, executive trainers can point during seminars to Henry Ford as an example of a leader without fear of being challenged.

Leadership as ethical action requires that both means and ends serve the common good. Companies are beginning to realize what a powerful combination this is. Gandhi, King and others knew it a long time ago. If businesses can resist the temptation to use values to boost efficiency rather than increasing efficiency to serve values, everyone will benefit. Both the process and the product have to be ethical. In the business world, managers build companies, but leaders influence followers to join them in building a better world.

Locating leadership theory within ethical theory also helps us answer some perennial questions. *Can leadership exist without management?* No. Management is a tool, and leaders will always need to use it. *What about vice versa?* Yes. Management can flourish entirely independently of leadership. It does so when it serves an individual's needs or desires, or those of a group, without regard for the common good. *Can leadership be taught?* Only to the extent that ethics can be taught. *Can ethics be taught?* Partially. People can learn, be taught, or be shown what ought to be done, and can be shown how to make decisions about what ought to be done. But they cannot be made to do what ought to be done. The strength to do that can only come from true meaning and purpose. *Does private behavior have anything to do with leadership?* Yes. One's private behavior must be consistent with the ethical principles involved in the leadership project. If not, the leadership relation is in jeopardy. Ethical principles are violated if limited to a particular context. *Was Hitler a leader?* No, because he did not use ethical means, and because his goals served an exclusively German Volkish idea rather than the common good.[6]

One question we don't often hear (but should hear *all* the time) in academic discussions of leadership is this: *What about Abraham Maslowe's hierarchy of needs and Lawrence Kohlberg's stages of moral development?* The difference is subtle, but one fits here and the other doesn't. Kohlberg's point is very similar to the point being made in this book. Leaders exhibit the highest level of moral development by going beyond both pre-conventional (service to self) and conventional (service to their own group or society) levels of moral reasoning to pursue post-conventional principles (service to all). Kohlberg's highest level reaches out to meet each of Maslowe's levels of need, but in return Maslowe is free to dispense with Kohlberg. Leaders apply Kohlberg when they operate at the highest level of moral reasoning and help to meet others' genuine needs, but Maslowe's self-esteem, self-efficacy and social esteem needs can be pursued and served (though in a corrupt manner) by simply amassing power.

The previous chapter suggested that leadership could be defined as the art of guiding followers in collaborative pursuit of a mutually understood aspect of the common good. Whether or not this is the best way to organize them, there are important elements here that seem always to be essential. Leadership is an art (not a science).[7] It involves guidance by the leader, but followers contribute to and influence the course taken as they collaborate with the leader and other followers. It involves activity aimed at somehow serving a mutually understood and accepted aspect of the common good (as opposed to just individual or collective goods). This definition implicitly excludes coercion or manipulation, and separates the leadership relation from the necessarily preceding operation of influence alone. (Leadership occurs after influence has done its initial work, not before, and influence continues to operate in the leadership relation.)

But this is a highly sterile, technical analysis of a process that cannot be empirically measured or verified. More practically, the only thing that ultimately distinguishes management from leadership is the element of the common good. The common good, admittedly, is sometimes extremely hard to define, but that is no excuse to avoid it. A recent *Time* magazine cover bears a picture of an eleven-year-old African girl with AIDS. The caption reads, "This is a story about AIDS in Africa. Look at the pictures. Read the words. And then try not to care."

We usually don't need a highly technical definition of the common good. Opportunities to serve the common good are staring us in the face, if we will raise our eyes to them. What we lack is the courage, commitment and consideration for others to do so, which is ironic in light of how much we have at our disposal. We live in a world where there are many obvious needs, but at the same time there exist tremendous resources of many kinds that could be brought to bear on those needs.

Leadership is a critical link between resources and needs. What keeps us from leading? Each of us must answer that question for ourselves, but I would suggest that Frankl speaks to everyone when he talks of responsibility. We must seek meaning responsibly, and then be responsible to the meaning we find. But even those who find meaning have trouble staying entirely clear of the survival paradigm. That is, we are all awash in the market ocean, and the market, being a product of that paradigm, wants us to buy and consume as much as possible no matter what else that prevents us (or others) from doing. We invest far too many resources in products we really don't need, consuming too conspicuously, too often, too much. This keeps us from more important things. Martin Luther King, Jr. put it in starker terms.

> *Every man must decide whether he will walk in the light of creative altruism or in the darkness of destructive selfishness. Life's most persistent and urgent question is, What are you doing for others?*[8]

Perhaps we would be less apt to forget this truth if we changed the way we choose and use our words. For example, what if we made a conscious attempt to use the word "leadership" only when the activity in question served the common good? What if we took care not to say "leader" or "leadership" when "manager" or "management" is the more correct choice? Perhaps we would think a bit more about where we are going. Maybe our view of the forest would be a bit less obstructed by trees.

Given the global marketplace, large multinational corporations, global communication networks, and increasing ease of international travel, leadership as service to the common good is a definition for our times. We really are one community now. What is good is common.

Notes

PROLOGUE

1. Leadership theorist Joanne Ciulla represents the academic view. She asserts that Rost's claim that "what leadership studies needs is a common definition of leadership" is off the mark. Ciulla, Joanne B., "Leadership Ethics: Mapping the Territory," in Joanne B. Ciulla, ed., *Ethics, The Heart of Leadership* (Westport, CT: Praeger, 1998), p. 10.
2. George F. Will, *Statecraft as Soulcraft: What Government Does* (New York: Simon & Schuster, 1983), p. 47.
3. Ibid., p. 49.
4. From a speech delivered at Peoria, Illinois in 1854. Cited in Will, pp. 47-48.

Chapter 1 LEADERSHIP AND ETHICS

1. J.M. Burns, *Leadership* (New York: HarperCollins, 1978), p. 20. Burns occasionally used the term "transformational" instead, but the latter term came into common use primarily as a result of the work of leadership theorist Bernard Bass. Although Bass's approach differs from that of Burns in important ways, some scholars now use the two terms interchangeably.
2. Robert K. Greenleaf, *Servant Leadership: A Journey into the Nature of Legitimate Power and Greatness* (New York: Paulist Press, 1977).
3. Joanne B. Ciulla, ed., *Ethics, The Heart of Leadership* (Westport, CT: Praeger, 1998), p. 10.
4. Ibid., back cover.
5. Ibid.
6. Ibid., p. 3.
7. Ciulla correctly points out that the distinction between ethics and morals is not particularly significant to most philosophers.

8. More exactly, ethics, along with aesthetics, is a category under "axiology," which in turn is a category under philosophy, but all three are now commonly referred to together simply as "ethics."
9. These latter two are rarely invoked in the leadership literature, but perhaps they should be more often. Christopher Hodgkinson has cogently argued that leaders are in essence philosophers because they deal with "why" questions. See Hodgkinson, *The Philosophy of Leadership* (Oxford, England: Basil Blackwell, 1983).
10. Cited in Hamilton, James R. et.al. *Readings for an Introduction to Philosophy* (New York: Macmillan, 1976), p. 1.
11. For a discussion of the way paradigms may function in science, see Thomas Kuhn, *The Structure of Scientific Revolutions* (Chicago, IL: University of Chicago Press, 1962).
12. Burns, pp. 75-76.
13. Here it is: "Leadership over human beings is exercised when persons with certain motives and purposes mobilize, in competition or conflict with others, institutional, political, psychological, and other resources so as to arouse, engage, and satisfy the motives of followers." Ibid., p. 18.
14. Joseph C. Rost, *Leadership for the Twenty-First Century* (New York: Praeger, 1991), p. 102.
15. For Rost's judgment of Burns's concept of "transforming leadership," see ibid., p. 165.
16. Ibid., p. 161.
17. Ibid., pp. 165-166.
18. Greenleaf, pp. 13-14.

Chapter 2 WORLDS OF SURVIVAL

1. David M. Buss, *The Evolution of Desire* (New York: BasicBooks, 1994), p. 17. In Ashley Montagu's words, "Next to the Bible no work has been quite as influential, in virtually every aspect of human thought, as *The Origin of Species*." This statement appears on the back cover of the 1958 Mentor edition of *Origin*.
2. Lesslie Newbigin, *Foolishness to the Greeks* (Grand Rapids, MI: Eerdmans, 1986).
3. Daniel J. Boorstin, *The Discoverers* (New York: Random House, 1983), p. 407.
4. Buss, pp. 14 and 17.
5. Ibid., p. 17.
6. Ibid., inside back cover.
7. Thomas Hobbes, *Leviathan* (New York: Simon & Schuster, 1964 [1651]), p. 85.

8. Ibid., pp. 82-86.
9. "Conflicts rage in more than one-third of nations." Lawrence Journal-World, Washington AP wire story, December 30, 2000, page 3A.
10. Hodgkinson, pp. 58-59.
11. Charles Darwin, *The Origin of Species* (New York: New American Library, 1958 [1859]), p. 450. Darwin had his doubts, however. "What a book a devil's chaplain might write on the clumsy, wasteful, blundering, low and horribly cruel works of nature!" Cited in Gertrude Himmelfarb, *Darwin and the Darwinian Revolution* (Garden City, New York: Doubleday, 1959), p. 329.
12. Julian Huxley, *Religion Without Revelation* (New York: Harper & Row, 1957), p. 194.
13. Hodgkinson, pp. 58, 60, and 61.
14. Ibid., p. 65.
15. Newbigin, p. 31.
16. Ibid.
17. Ibid.
18. As anyone who has read him knows, Nietzsche's writing is highly stylized and idiosyncratic, and thus extremely difficult to distill or outline. No claim is made that the attempt to do so herein is either comprehensive or without error.
19. William Hubben, *Dostoevsky, Kierkegaard, Nietzsche, and Kafka: Four Prophets of Our Destiny* (New York: Collier, 1962 [1952]).
20. Friedrich Nietzsche, *The Gay Science*, aphorism 4. Reprinted in Walter Kaufmann, ed., *The Portable Nietzsche* (New York: Penguin, 1982 [1954]). pp. 93-94.
21. Neitzsche, Friedrich. *Beyond Good and Evil: Prelude to a Philosophy of the Future*. Translated, with commentary, by Walter Kaufmann (New York: Random House, 1966), pp. 291-292.
22. Hubben, p. 114.
23. Nietzsche, *Beyond Good and Evil*, aphorism 212. Reprinted in Kaufmann, *Portable Nietzsche*, p. 446.
24. Hubben, p. 106 and 112.
25. Nietzsche, *The Gay Science*, aphorism 343. Reprinted in Kaufmann, *Portable Nietzsche*, pp. 447-448.
26. Nietzsche, *Nietzsche contra Wagner* (*We Antipodes*). Ibid., p. 670.
27. [1] Nietzsche, *Twilight of the Idols*, aphorism 38. Ibid., p. 539.
28. John Keegan, *The Mask of Command* (New York: Viking Penguin, 1987), pp. 254-255.
29. Hubben.
30. Neitzsche, Friedrich. *Beyond Good and Evil: Prelude to a Philosophy of the Future*, p. 292.

31. Nietzsche, *The Gay Science*, aphorism 344, in Kaufmann, *Portable Nietzsche*, pp. 449-450.
32. Ironically, modern physicists are more likely to argue for purpose (despite Newton's laws) and the natural scientists for a lack thereof (despite Darwin's faith). See for example John C. Polkinghorne, *Faith, Science, and Understanding* (New Haven, CN: Yale University Press, 2000).
33. Boorstin, p. 452.
34. Newbigin, 35.
35. Quoted in David Friend and eds., *The Meaning of Life* (Boston, MA: Little, Brown and Company, 1991), p. 33. It should perhaps be pointed out here that Gould, in asserting that something does not exist, is committing a fundamental logical error. In order to prove conclusively that something does not exist, one must have exhaustive knowledge of the universe. It is much more defensible—because it is much more logically credible—to say that certain evidence leads one to *believe* that something does not exist.
36. Stephen Hawking, lecture delivered at Cambridge University, quoted in R. Zacharias, *The Veritas Forum at Harvard University*, lectures delivered in 1992. Hawking's sentiments suggest another way of interpreting Julian Huxley's statement that "as a result of Darwin's work...light has been thrown on [man's] destiny." This statement appears on the back cover of the 1958 Mentor edition of Darwin's *Origin of Species*.
37. Lawrence Journal-World, January 15, 2001, p. 2A.
38. Friend, ibid.

Chapter 3   MANAGING TO SURVIVE

1. Kohlberg, Lawrence. *The Philosophy of Moral Development: Essays on Moral Development, Volume I* (New York: Harper & Row, 1981).
2. It is interesting to note that Taylor in fact referred to his system as "scientific management." The fact that it was "scientific" was used in those days to justify it against any moral objections that might be raised against it. See Mary Midgley, "Visions of Embattled Science," in Ronald Barnett and Anne Griffin, eds., *The End of Knowledge in Higher Education* (London: Redwood Books, 1997), p. 69.
3. Ibid.
4. Hodgkinson, p. 97.
5. Ibid., p. 135.
6. Burns, p. 258.
7. Hodgkinson, p. 97.
8. Wm. E. Rosenbach and Robert L.Taylor, eds., 4th ed., *Contemporary Issues in Leadership* (Boulder, CO: Westview Press, 1998), pp. 8 & 9.

9. James M. Kouzes and Barry Z. Posner, *The Leadership Challenge: How to Keep Getting Extraordinary Things Done in Organizations*, 2nd ed., (San Francisco, CA: Jossey-Bass, 1995), p. 39.
10. Rost, p. 161.
11. Hodgkinson, p. 164.
12. Ibid., p. 133.
13. Kouzes and Posner, p. 131.
14. Ibid., p. 30.
15. In Ciulla, p. x.
16. Hodgkinson, p. 161.
17. Hubben, p. 114.
18. Hubben, p. 119.
19. Nietzsche, *Nietzsche contra Wagner*, in Kaufmann, *Portable Nietzsche*, p. 671.
20. Nietzsche, *The Gay Science*, excerpted in Walter Kaufmann, ed., *Existentialism from Dostoevsky to Sartre* (Cleveland, OH: World, 1956), p. 104.
21. Hodgkinson says something similar regarding administrators: "Organization is the canvas of the administrative art." Hodgkinson, p. 2.
22. Ibid., p. 88. For representative translated excerpts from the *Arthasastra* itself, see Lynn H. Nelson and Patrick Peebles, eds., *Classics of Eastern Thought* (New York: Harcourt Brace Jovanovich, 1991), pp. 81-90.
23. This is what Nietzsche meant by the "annihilation of morality". Not destroying morality entirely, but reducing it to the role of a tool. Nietzsche, *Ecce Homo*, in Kaufmann, *Existentialism*, p. 111.
24. In Nietzsche's own words, "To give style to one's character—a great and rare art!" This is the phrase from Nietzsche upon which Badaracco builds his argument. Joseph L. Badaracco, Jr., *Defining Moments: When Managers Must Choose Between Right and Right* (Boston, MA: Harvard Business School Press, 1997), p. 70.
25. Gerald R. Griffin, *Machiavelli on Management: Playing and Winning the Corporate Power Game* (New York: Praeger, 1991), p. xi.
26. Jeffrey Pfeffer, *Managing With Power: Politics and Influence in Organizations* (Boston, MA: Harvard Business School Press, 1992), p. 342.
27. Ibid., p. 342.
28. James MacGregor Burns and Georgia J. Sorenson, *Dead Center: Clinton-Gore Leadership and the Perils of Moderation* (New York: Scribner, 1999), p. 50.
29. Thomas L. Friedman, *The Lexus and the Olive Tree: Understanding Globalization* (New York: Farrar, Strauss and Giroux, 1999).

Chapter 4   A WORLD OF PURPOSE

1. Nancy Pearcey, "Singer in the Rain," in *First Things*, no. 106, October 2000, p. 62.
2. Darwin to Asa Gray, April 3, 1860: *Life and Letters*, II, 296. Cited in Himmelfarb, p. 330.
3. Charles Darwin, "Autobiography," In de Beer, Gavin, ed. *Charles Darwin and T.H. Huxley: Autobiographies* (New York: Oxford University Press, 1984 [1876]), p. 54.
4. Himmelfarb, p. 330.
5. Peter Singer, *A Darwinian Left: Politics, Evolution, and Cooperation* (New Haven, CT: Yale University Press, 2000), pp. 62-63.
6. Ironically, it is the capacity to "reason" that Peter Singer believes can take human beings beyond the constraints of Darwinism to altruism. He takes this position despite having rejected the existence of *a reason why* altruism is to be preferred over natural selection. That is, he trusts we will reason without (a) reason.
7. Richard Dawkins, "Forever Voyaging: The Genius of W.D. Hamilton, 1936-2000," *Times Literary Supplement*, August 4, 2000, p. 12.
8. See Ullica Segerstrale, *Defenders of the Truth: The Battle for Science in the Sociobiology Debate and Beyond* (New York: Oxford, 2000).
9. Stephen Jay Gould, "Darwin's More Stately Mansion," in *Science*, vol. 284, June 25, 1999, p. 2087.
10. Wilson, Edward O. *Consilience* (New York: Knopf, 1998), p. 258. Wilson states that the central idea of the consilience world view is "that all tan-gible phenomena, from the birth of the stars to the workings of social institutions, are based on material processes that are ultimately reducible, however long and tortuous the sequences, to the laws of physics." *Consilience*, p. 266.
11. Nietzsche, *Schopenhauer as Educator*, in Kaufmann, *Existentialism*, p. 103.
12. Viktor E. Frankl, *The Will to Meaning: Foundations and Applications of Logotherapy* (Cleveland, OH: World, 1969), p. 54.
13. Some will recognize here Frankl's intentional appropriation of Nietzschean phraseology to entitle a book that expresses the antithesis of Nietzsche's worldview. Against the atheist German philosopher's will to power in the absence of purpose, the theist German psychiatrist opposes his own will to meaning in recognition of purpose.
14. Ibid., p. 60.
15. Louis Dupre, *Symbols of the Sacred* (Grand Rapids, MI: Eerdman's, 2000).
16. Frankl, pp. 55 and 60.
17. Excerpted from the Fall 2000 convocation address of Dr. Robert Hemenway, Chancellor of the University of Kansas, Lawrence, KS, August 23, 2000.

18. John M. Bryson and Barbara C. Crosby, *Leadership for the Common Good: Tackling Public Problems in a Shared-Power World* (San Francisco, CA: Jossey-Bass, 1992), p. 358.
19. Further discussion in this direction might begin by comparing the definition here to political theorist John Rawls's conception of the common good as "certain general conditions that are in an appropriate sense equally to everyone's advantage."
20. Ibid., p. 357.
21. J. Thomas Wren, "James Madison and the Ethics of Transformational Leadership," in Ciulla, p. 147.
22. Burns, p. 43. Italics in original.
23. Ibid., p. 240. It is instructive to compare the American revolution in this respect to others. For an enlightening comparison of the English, American, French and Russian revolutions, see Crane Brinton, *The Anatomy of Revolution* (New York: Random House, 1965 [1938]), rev. ed.
24. Abram T. Collier, "Business Leadership and a Creative Society," reprinted in *Harvard Business Review*, vol. 46, no. 1, Jan-Feb 1968 [Jan-Feb 1953], p. 155.
25. For a disturbing and sobering examination of the significance of such decisions, see Christopher Browning's *Ordinary Men: Reserve Police Battalion 101 and the Final Solution in Poland* (New York: HarperCollins, 1993).

Chapter 5 LEADERSHIP: ~~SURVIVAL~~ SERVICE OF THE ~~FITTEST~~ FAITHFUL

1. Robert Coles, *Lives of Moral Leadership* (New York: Random House, 2000), p. xiv.
2. Ibid., xv-xvi.
3. Gilbert Fairholm, *Values Leadership: Toward a New Philosophy of Leadership* (New York: Praeger, 1991), p. 45.
4. Greenleaf, pp. 13-14.
5. Burns, pp. 429 and 433.
6. Ibid., p. 20.
7. John W. Gardner, *On Leadership* (New York: Free Press, 1990), pp. 76 and 77.
8. Ibid., pp. 95 and 97.
9. Howard Gardner, *Leading Minds: An Anatomy of Leadership* (New York: BasicBooks, 1995), pp. 55 and 56.
10. Hodgkinson, pp. 228 and 229.
11. Peter F. Drucker, *Post-Capitalist Society* (New York: HarperCollins, 1993), p. 102.

12. Ibid., p. 109
13. Kouzes and Posner, pp. 131, 132 and 133.
14. Bernard M. Bass, "The Ethics of Transformational Leadership," in Ciulla, p. 171.
15. Coles, p. xi.
16. Ciulla, xv.
17. Rost, p. 153.
18. Ibid., pp. 173 and 175.
19. Ibid., p. 177.
20. John Dalla Costa, *The Ethical Imperative: Why Moral Leadership is Good Business* (Reading, MA: Addison-Wesley, 1998), p. 239.
21. Rost, p. 161.
22. Al Gini, "Moral Leadership and Business Ethics," in Ciulla, p. 37.
23. Kouzes and Posner, p. 30.
24. Tom Peters and B. Waterman, *In Search of Excellence* (New York: Harper & Row, 1982), p. 26. This is the way Rosenbach and Taylor paraphrase it. Wm. E. Rosenbach and Robert L. Taylor, *Contemporary Issues in Leadership* (Boulder, CO: Westview Press, 1998), 4th ed., p. 8. In fact, Peters and Waterman referred specifically to the "chief executive" rather than to leadership in general.
25. Rosenbach and Taylor, p. 1.
26. John Gardner, p. 1.
27. Al Gini in Rosenbach and Taylor, p. 7.
28. Fairholm, p. 44.
29. Rost, p. 126.
30. Hodgkinson, p. 31.
31. The relationship between leadership and power is an important topic not taken up here. John Kenneth Galbraith's discussion of "conditioned power" suggests an interesting basis for contrasting power that depends on persuasion or belief (conscious or unconscious) with the understanding of leadership argued for herein. See J. K. Galbraith, *The Anatomy of Power* (Boston, MA: Houghton Mifflin, 1983).
32. "Reason" here refers not to the capacity to reason (think), but to the synonym for purpose, an answer to the question, "Why?"
33. Drucker, p. 101.
34. Hodgkinson, p. 32.
35. Hyrum W. Smith, *The 10 Natural Laws of Successful Time and Life Management* (New York: Warner Books, 1995), pp. 69-70.
36. Burns, p. 19.
37. "A Gore bid in 2004 a long shot," Lawrence Journal World, December 14, 2000, p. 7A.

38. "Clinton years a lost opportunity," Lawrence Journal World, January 14, 2001, p. 6B.
39. "Clinton gives 1st farewell address," ABC News-Washington Post poll, Lawrence Journal World, January 19, 2001, p. 5A.
40. *Agenda* interview with Chris Gunness, BBC World Radio, October 28, 2000.
41. Cited by Jim Lehrer et.al., PBS election night live broadcast, November 7, 2000.
42. Burns & Sorenson, pp. 290-291.
43. Ibid., p. 278.
44. Ibid.
45. PBS election night live broadcast, November 7, 2000.
46. Burns & Sorenson, p. 277. Italics added.
47. Clinton's last days as President will be forever remembered due to the string of dubious pardons he granted. Those are not discussed here because direct links between one or more of the pardons and earlier political favors have yet to be proven. Time and ongoing investigations may tell whether or not these were acts of survival as well, or the logical conclusion to Clinton's style of "transactional leadership."
48. "Clinton cuts deal to avoid prosecution," Lawrence Journal World, January 20, 2001, p. 6A.
49. "Clinton gives 1st farewell address," Lawrence Journal World, January 19, 2001, p. 5A.
50. Rosenbach and Taylor, p. xii.
51. Bass, in Ciulla, p. 173.
52. Joseph L. Badaracco, Jr. and Richard R. Ellsworth, *Leadership and the Quest for Integrity* (Boston, MA: Harvard Business School Press, 1989), p. 106.
53. Ibid., p. 73.
54. Robert E. Kelley, *The Power of Followership* (New York: Doubleday, 1992), p. 169.
55. Wren, p. 151.
56. Manuel Velaszquez, "International Business, Morality, and the Common Good," *Business Ethics Quarterly*, vol. 2, issue 1 (July 1992): 27-40. Reprinted in Joseph DesJardins & John McCall, *Contemporary Issues in Business Ethics* (Belmont, CA: Wadsworth, 2000), p. 520.
57. Ibid., p. 519.
58. DeGeorge, Richard T. *Competing With Integrity in International Business* (New York: Oxford University Press, 1993).
59. A compact but useful text is Gregory Beabout and Daryl Wennemann's *Applied Professional Ethics: A Developmental Approach for Use with Case Studies* (Lanham, MD: University Press of America, 1994)

60. Badaracco.
61. "13-year-old blames pro wrestling for girl's death," Lawrence Journal World, January 17, 2001, p. 3A.
62. "XFL game geared to extreme tastes," Lawrence Journal World, January 28, 2001, p. 8B.
63. "Youth violence linked to media exposure," Lawrence Journal World, January 17, 2001, p. 3A.
64. Drucker, p. 101.
65. Newbigin, p. 114.
66. Bill Fuerst, Dean of Business, University of Kansas, interview published in Fall 2000 *Accolades*, University of Kansas Alumni Association.
67. DeGeorge, p. 194.
68. Paul Ramsey, *Fabricated Man: The Ethics of Genetic Control* (New Haven, CT: Yale University Press, 1970), p. 13.
69. James F. Autry, *Life & Work: A Manager's Search for Meaning* (New York: Wm. Morrow and Co., 1994), p. 255.
70. Ibid., p. 241.
71. See for example evolutionary psychologist Buss's discussion of the impact of marital discord and divorce on the later lives of children. Buss, p. 217.

Chapter 6 *HOW DO LEADERS SURVIVE?*

1. National Public Radio, *Morning Edition* interview with Susan Stamberg, October 24, 2000.
2. "Gopher coach avoids temptation," Sam Donnellon, Philadelphia Daily News. Reprinted in the Lawrence Journal World, July 14, 2000.
3. Burns, p. 107.
4. Kathryn Spink, *Mother Teresa: A Complete Authorized Biography* (New York: HarperCollins, 1997), pp. 55-56.
5. John Gardner, p. xii.
6. For a fascinating study of the Volkish idea that had much to do with the birth of German fascism, see George L. Mosse, *The Crisis of German Ideology: Intellectual Origins of the Third Reich* (New York: Grosset and Dunlap, 1964).
7. See Max De Pree's excellent little book, *Leadership is an Art* (East Lansing, MI: Michigan State University Press, 1987).
8. Cited in Robert K. Cooper and Ayman Sawaf, *Executive EQ: Emotional Intelligence in Leadership and Organizations* (New York: Berkley, 1997), p. 204.

Bibliography

Atkins, Peter. "Will Science Ever Fail?" in *New Scientist, August 8, 1992.*

Autry, James F. *Life & Work: A Manager's Search for Meaning* (New York: Wm. Morrow and Co., 1994).

Badaracco, Joseph L. Jr. *Defining Moments: When Managers Must Choose Between Right and Right* (Boston, MA: Harvard Business School Press, 1997).

Badaracco, Joseph L. Jr. and Ellsworth, Richard R. *Leadership and the Quest for Integrity* (Boston, MA: Harvard Business School Press, 1989).

Bass, Bernard M. "The Ethics of Transformational Leadership," in Ciulla, pp. 169-192.

Beabout, Gregory R. and Wennemann, Daryl J. *Applied Professional Ethics: A Developmental Approach for Use with Case Studies* (Lanham, MD: University Press of America, 1994).

Beck, Robert N. and Orr, John B. *Ethical Choice: A Case Study Approach* (New York: Free Press, 1970).

Bethell, Tom. "Against Sociobiology," *First Things* 109 (Jan. 2001), pp. 18-24.

Boorstin, Daniel J. *The Discoverers* (New York: Random House, 1983).

Brinton, Crane. *The Anatomy of Revolution* (New York: Random House, 1965 [1938]), rev. ed.

Browning, Christopher R. *Ordinary Men: Reserve Police Battalion 101 and the Final Solution in Poland* (New York: HarperCollins, 1993).

Bryson, John M. and Crosby, Barbara C. *Leadership for the Common Good: Tackling Public Problems in a Shared-Power World* (San Francisco, CA: Jossey-Bass, 1992).

BIBLIOGRAPHY

Burns, James MacGregor. *Leadership* (New York: HarperCollins, 1978).

Burns, James MacGregor and Sorenson, Georgia J. *Dead Center: Clinton-Gore Leadership and the Perils of Moderation* (New York: Scribner, 1999).

Buss, David M. *The Evolution of Desire* (New York: BasicBooks, 1994).

Ciulla, Joanne B., ed. *Ethics, The Heart of Leadership* (Westport, CT: Praeger, 1998).

Coles, Robert. *Lives of Moral Leadership* (New York: Random House, 2000).

Collier, Abram T. "Business Leadership and a Creative Society," reprinted in *Harvard Business Review*, vol. 46, no. 1, Jan-Feb 1968 [Jan-Feb 1953].

Cooper, Robert K. and Sawaf, Ayman. *Executive EQ: Emotional Intelligence in Leadership and Organizations* (New York: Berkley, 1997).

Dalla Costa, John. *The Ethical Imperative: Why Moral Leadership is Good Business* (Reading, MA: Addison-Wesley, 1998).

Darwin, Charles. *The Origin of Species* (New York: New American Library, 1958 [1859]).

_____. *Autobiography*. In de Beer, Gavin, ed. *Charles Darwin and T.H. Huxley: Autobiographies* (New York: Oxford University Press, 1984 [1876]).

Dawkins, Richard. *The Blind Watchmaker* (New York: Norton, 1987).

_____. "Forever Voyaging: The Genius of W.D. Hamilton, 1936-2000," *Times Literary Supplement*, August 4, 2000, pp. 12-13.

DeGeorge, Richard T. *Competing With Integrity in International Business* (New York: Oxford University Press, 1993).

De Pree, Max. *Leadership is an Art* (East Lansing, MI: Michigan State University Press, 1987).

DesJardins, Joseph & McCall, John. *Contemporary Issues in Business Ethics* (Belmont, CA: Wadsworth, 2000).

Drucker, Peter F. *Post-Capitalist Society* (New York: HarperCollins, 1993).

Dupre, Louis. *Symbols of the Sacred* (Grand Rapids, MI: Eerdman's, 2000).

Fairholm, Gilbert. *Values Leadership: Toward a New Philosophy of Leadership* (New York: Praeger, 1991).

Frankl, Viktor E. *The Will to Meaning: Foundations and Applications of Logotherapy* (Cleveland, OH: World, 1969).

Friedman, Thomas L. *The Lexus and the Olive Tree: Understanding Globalization* (New York: Farrar, Strauss and Giroux, 1999).

Friend, David and eds. *The Meaning of Life* (Boston, MA: Little, Brown and Company, 1991).

Galbraith, John Kenneth. *The Anatomy of Power* (Boston, MA: Houghton Mifflin, 1983).

Gardner, Howard. *Leading Minds: An Anatomy of Leadership* (New York: BasicBooks, 1995).

Gardner, John W. *On Leadership* (New York: Free Press, 1990).

Gini, Al. "Moral Leadership: An Overview," in Rosenbach and Taylor, pp. 5-16.

_____. "Moral Leadership and Business Ethics," in Ciulla, pp. 27-45.

Greenleaf, Robert K. *Servant Leadership: A Journey into the Nature of Legitimate Power and Greatness* (New York: Paulist Press, 1977).

Griffin, Gerald R. *Machiavelli on Management: Playing and Winning the Corporate Power Game* (New York: Praeger, 1991).

Gould, Stephen Jay. "Darwin's More Stately Mansion," in *Science*, vol. 284, June 25, 1999, p. 2087.

Hamilton, James R. et. al. *Readings for an Introduction to Philosophy* (New York: Macmillan, 1976).

Himmelfarb, Gertrude. *Darwin and the Darwinian Revolution* (Garden City, New York: Doubleday, 1959).

Hobbes, Thomas. Leviathan (New York: Simon & Schuster, 1964 [1651]).

Hodgkinson, Christopher. *Educational Leadership: The Moral Art* (Albany, NY: State University of New York Press, 1991).

_____. *The Philosophy of Leadership* (Oxford, England: Basil Blackwell, 1983).

Hubben, William. *Dostoevsky, Kierkegaard, Nietzsche, and Kafka: Four Prophets of Our Destiny* (New York: Collier, 1962 [1952]).

Hunt, Arnold D., *Ethics of World Religions* (San Diego, CA: Greenhaven Press, 1991), rev. ed.

Huxley, Julian. *Religion Without Revelation*, rev. ed. (New York: Harper & Row1957).

Kaufmann, Walter, ed. *Existentialism from Dostoevsky to Sartre* (Cleveland, OH: World, 1956).

_____, ed. *The Portable Nietzsche* (New York: Penguin, 1982 [1954]).

Kelley, Robert E. *The Power of Followership* (New York: Doubleday, 1992).

Kohlberg, Lawrence. *The Philosophy of Moral Development: Essays on Moral Development, Volume I* (New York: Harper & Row, 1981).

Kouzes, James M. and Posner, Barry Z. *The Leadership Challenge: How to Keep Getting Extraordinary Things Done in Organizations*, 2nd ed. (San Francisco, CA: Jossey-Bass, 1995).

Midgley, Mary. "Visions of Embattled Science," in Barnett, Ronald and Griffin, Anne, eds. *The End of Knowledge in Higher Education* (London: Redwood Books, 1997).

Mosse, George L. *The Crisis of German Ideology: Intellectual Origins of the Third Reich* (New York: Grosset and Dunlap, 1964).

Mullen, John Douglas. *Kierkegaard's Philosophy: Self-Deception and Cowardice in the Present Age* (New York: New American Library, 1981).

Neitzsche, Friedrich. *Beyond Good and Evil: Prelude to a Philosophy of the Future*. Translated, with Commentary, by Walter Kaufmann (New York: Random House, 1966).

Nelson, Lynn H. and Peebles, Patrick, eds. *Classics of Eastern Thought* (New York: Harcourt Brace Jovanovich, 1991).

Newbigin, Lesslie. *Foolishness to the Greeks* (Grand Rapids, MI: Eerdmans, 1986).

Pfeffer, Jeffrey. *Managing With Power: Politics and Influence in Organizations* (Boston, MA: Harvard Business School Press, 1992).

Polkinghorne, John C. *Faith, Science, and Understanding* (New Haven, CN: Yale University Press, 2000).

Ramsey, Paul. *Fabricated Man: The Ethics of Genetic Control* (New Haven, CT: Yale University Press, 1970).

Rosenbach, Wm. E. and Taylor, Robert L., eds., 4th ed. *Contemporary Issues in Leadership* (Boulder, CO: Westview Press, 1998).

Rost, Joseph C. *Leadership for the Twenty-First Century* (New York: Praeger, 1991).

Scott, Sir Walter. Author's Introduction to *Ivanhoe* (New York: TAB, 1959 [1830]).

Segerstrale, Ullica. *Defenders of the Truth: The Battle for Science in the Sociobiology Debate and Beyond* (New York: Oxford, 2000).

Singer, Peter. *A Darwinian Left: Politics, Evolution, and Cooperation* (New Haven, CT: Yale University Press, 2000).

Smith, Hyrum W. *The 10 Natural Laws of Successful Time and Life Management* (New York: Warner Books, 1995).

Spink, Kathryn. *Mother Teresa: A Complete Authorized Biography* (New York: HarperCollins, 1997).

Velaszquez, Manuel. "International Business, Morality, and the Common Good," *Business Ethics Quarterly*, vol. 2, issue 1 (July 1992): 27-40. Reprinted in Joseph DesJardins & John McCall, *Contemporary Issues in Business Ethics* (Belmont, CA: Wadsworth, 2000), pp. 512-521.

Will, George F. *Statecraft as Soulcraft: What Government Does* (New York: Simon & Schuster, 1983).

Wilson, Edward O. *Consilience* (New York: Knopf, 1998).

Wren, J.Thomas. "James Madison and the Ethics of Transformational Leadership," in Ciulla, pp. 145-168.